Debt Recovery

Cavendish
Publishing
Limited

London • Sydney • Portland, Oregon

Debt Recovery

Mark Fairweather & Rosy Border

Cavendish
Publishing
Limited

London • Sydney • Portland, Oregon

Second edition first published in Great Britain 2004 by
Cavendish Publishing Limited, The Glass House,
Wharton Street, London WC1X 9PX, United Kingdom
Telephone: + 44 (0)20 7278 8000   Facsimile: + 44 (0)20 7278 8080
Email: info@cavendishpublishing.com
Website: www.cavendishpublishing.com

Published in the United States by Cavendish Publishing
c/o International Specialized Book Services,
5824 NE Hassalo Street, Portland,
Oregon 97213-3644, USA

Published in Australia by Cavendish Publishing (Australia) Pty Ltd
45 Beach Street, Coogee, NSW 2034, Australia
Email: info@cavendishpublishing.com.au
Website: www.cavendishpublishing.com.au

The first edition of this title was originally published by The Stationery Office

British Library Cataloguing in Publication Data
Fairweather, Mark
Debt Recovery – 2nd ed – (Pocket lawyer)
1 Collection laws – England 2 Collection laws – Wales
I Title II Border, Rosy

Library of Congress Cataloguing in Publication Data
Data available

ISBN 1-85941-858-9

1 3 5 7 9 10 8 6 4 2

Printed and bound in Great Britain

Contents

Disclaimer

This book puts *you* in control. This is an excellent thing, but it also makes *you* responsible for using it properly. Few washing machine manufacturers will honour their guarantee if you don't follow their 'instructions for use'. In the same way, we are unable to accept liability for any loss arising from mistakes or misunderstandings on your part. So take time to read this book carefully.

Although this book points you in the right direction, reading one small book will not make you an expert, and there are times when you may need to take advice from professionals. This book is not a definitive statement of the law, although we believe it to be accurate as at November 2003.

The authors and publisher cannot accept liability for any advice or material that becomes obsolete due to subsequent changes in the law after publication, although every effort will be made to show any changes in the law that take place after the publication date on the companion website.

About the authors

Mark Fairweather is a practising solicitor, and is one of the founding partners of the legal firm Fairweather Stephenson & Co. He has co-written 14 books with Rosy Border, including five titles in Cavendish Publishing's *Pocket Lawyer*. He has two children and lives in Suffolk.

Rosy Border, co-author of this title and series editor of the *Pocket Lawyer* series, has a first class honours degree in French and has worked in publishing, lecturing, journalism and the law. A prolific author and adapter, she stopped counting after 150 titles. Rosy and her husband, John Rabson, live in rural Suffolk and have a grown up family. Rosy enjoys DIY, entertaining and retail therapy in French markets.

Acknowledgments

A glance at the 'Useful contacts' will show the many sources we dipped into while writing this book. Thank you, everybody. We would especially like to thank John Rabson, Chartered Engineer, for his IT support and refreshments.

Welcome

Welcome to *Pocket Lawyer*. Let's face it, the law is a maze and you are likely to get lost unless you have a map. This book is your map through the part of the maze that deals with getting your debtors to pay up. It contains everything lawyers would tell you about the subject, if only they had time (and you had the money to pay them).

We put *you* in control

This book empowers you. This is a good thing but being in control brings responsibility as well as power, so please use this book properly. Read it with care and don't be afraid to make notes – we have left wide margins for you to do just that. Take your time – do not skip anything:

○ everything is there for a purpose;

○ if anything were unimportant, we would have left it out.

Think of yourself as a driver using a road map. The map tells you the route, but it is up to you to drive carefully along it.

Sometimes you are in danger of getting out of your depth and you will need to take professional advice. Watch out for the hazard sign.

Sometimes we pause to explain something: the origin of a word, perhaps, or why a particular piece of legislation was passed. You do not need to know these things to make use of this book, but we hope you find them interesting.

Sometimes we stop to empower you to do something. Look out for the 'Power points' sign.

Clear English rules OK

Client to solicitor who has just drafted a contract for him: 'This *can't* be legal – I can understand it!'

Our style is WYSIWYG – what you see is what you get.

Some legal documents have traditionally been written in archaic language, often known as 'law-speak'. This term also extends to the practice of using the names of legal cases as shorthand for legal concepts. This wording has stood the test of time – often several centuries – and has been hallowed by the courts. Some of the words used sound just like everyday language, but beware – it is a kind of specialist shorthand. Since April 1999 the courts have made valiant efforts to modernise their language in an effort to become more user-friendly and encourage **litigants in person** (see 'Buzzwords'). For example, a 'plaintiff' has become a *claimant* and a 'summons' has become a *claim form*. There are still plenty of baffling terms, however. Many court forms, including some of the enforcement ones in this book, are still, at the time of writing, unmodernised: but have no fear! When we *do* need to use technical language, we offer clear explanations: see 'Buzzwords' below. These words appear in the text in **bold** so you can check their meaning.

A note on gender

This book is unisex. We acknowledge that there are both male and female members of every group and we try to allow for that in the text by using, wherever possible, the generic *they/them* rather than *he/she*, *him/her*, etc.

A note on Scotland and Northern Ireland

This book is not wholly reliable for jurisdictions other than England and Wales.

Click onto the website

www.cavendishpublishing.com/pocketlawyer

What this book can do for you

This book contains advice on:

o   avoiding debt problems in the first place;
o   the steps to take before starting legal action to recover a debt;
o   the legal options;
o   methods of enforcement – that is, actually getting the money after a court has ruled in your favour.

We give you:

o   the 'buzzwords' which are important in this section of the law and what they mean;
o   answers to some of the most frequently asked questions on the subject;
o   the paperwork you need:
    –   for a debt claim in the county court;
    –   to enforce a judgment debt;
    –   to bankrupt an individual;
    –   to put a company into liquidation;
o   sample letters requesting payment.

What this book can't do for you

It can't:

o   be a textbook. Its job is to help you to collect your debts, not teach you the ins and outs of contract law and court procedure (we aim to be streetwise rather than academic);

o   guarantee you will get your money;

o   replace specific advice you may need on your individual case;

o   work outside England and Wales – the law and court procedures are different even in Scotland and Northern Ireland (see 'A note on Scotland and Northern Ireland', above).

A word of encouragement

In an ideal world, your debtors would cave in and pay up after your first letter chasing payment. In our experience, this does happen quite often. If it happens to you, you are fortunate. It is, however, possible that at some time you will have to sue someone who owes you money. The court stage of debt recovery involves some serious form-filling – *don't be fazed by the forms.*

Forms were invented to set out at a glance information which might otherwise take a six-page letter, full of irrelevancies, to deliver. The court forms are designed to give the court the information it needs to handle your case in a format that officials can rapidly and easily understand.

While accuracy is important, form-filling is not an exact science and many people find it hard. Rosy (my co-author), in particular, complains bitterly that the 'space provided' is always the wrong size for what she wants to say, that she doesn't understand the questions, or that the instructions are ambiguous. She thinks too much, obviously!

Help is at hand for readers like Rosy.

- We explain the claim form, form N1, in detail. It is vital to get N1 right because it is the form you need to start off a claim for debt in the county court.
- We provide worked examples of a claim form, a bankruptcy petition and a winding-up petition.
- You can print off as many forms as you need from the Court Service website. This means you can have as many 'dry runs' as you wish (see our website for useful links). If you click onto the website accompanying this book, you'll find quick and easy links to the Court Service and Insolvency Service websites.
- Don't be afraid of telephoning or visiting the court – the officials are used to helping **litigants in person** (see 'Buzzwords') (and even lawyers who find forms difficult!) with the paperwork.
- Consider getting your completed paperwork checked by a court official before you file it. It's galling as well as time-wasting to have a good claim returned to you because you've ticked the wrong box or forgotten to sign the form.

If you have access to the internet you can make a claim for debt online using the Court Service's 'Money Claim Online' facility. This even calculates your court fee for you and lets you pay online by credit card. The main problem, from the point of view of the reluctant form-filler, is that computers are very literal-minded (see Chapter 5 for full details of this service – and the problem we encountered the first time we checked it out).

The websites you'll need

Court Service: www.courtservice.gov.uk

Department for Constitutional Affairs: www.dca.gov.uk *(note: this is the new name for the Lord Chancellor's Department)*

HM Land Registry: www.landreg.gov.uk

Insolvency Service: www.insolvency.gov.uk

Money Claim Online: www.courtservice.gov.uk/mcol

Buzzwords

Here are some terms you will come across in this book. Please do not skip this section, as many of the terms used by lawyers have special meanings. Here we make them clear. The terms appear in **bold** in the text.

acknowledgment of service – an interim reply by the *defendant* to a claim. The defendant signs and returns this form to the court to confirm that they have received the claim and intend to dispute it, and that they need more time to prepare their defence and/or *counterclaim*.

affidavit – a written statement of evidence.

An *affidavit* has to be signed by the witness and confirmed as true (sworn or affirmed) before a solicitor (who will charge £5) or a court official (who will do it for free). An affidavit is the written equivalent of spoken evidence given in the witness box. Since 26 April 1999, written evidence does not always have to be in affidavit form. We will let you know when an affidavit is required.

The word 'affidavit' comes from the Latin *affidare* – to declare (on oath) – and it means 'He, she or it has declared'. There. Now you can bore people at parties!

attachment of earnings order – a court order for a *judgment debt* to be paid by instalments out of the **debtor's** earnings from employment. Think of attachment of earnings as private PAYE with you as the taxman

bailiff – (in this context) a court official whose job includes collecting cash and/or seizing and selling goods, in payment of *judgment debts*.

When is a bailiff not a bailiff? When he (or she) is a 'sheriff's officer'. If you have a judgment against you which is being enforced in the High Court, a sheriff's officer rather than a bailiff will come knocking at your door. Neither can do so without a *warrant of execution*, however. Medieval, isn't it?

bankruptcy – the situation in which the court declares that a person (the *bankrupt*) cannot pay their debts, and that person's affairs are put into the hands of a *licensed insolvency practitioner*.

After a period of time, the bankrupt is allowed to keep all new earnings and all new assets. Unless the bankrupt has behaved badly, the slate is wiped clean except for assets which the debtor concealed from *creditors* and also certain debts (such as maintenance payments and state benefits which have been claimed dishonestly) to which bankruptcy does not apply (see Chapter 13).

charging order – a court order by which a *judgment debt* is secured against the debtor's home or other bricks and mortar.

Think of a charging order as a type of mortgage with you in the position of the lender, although you will not get paid by instalments; you have to wait until the property is sold before you get your money. You can also get a charging order on investment assets such as shares (see Chapter 12).

Civil Procedure Rules (CPR) – the rules everyone has to follow to conduct a court case. The main aim of the CPR is to enable the court 'to deal with cases justly'. The CPR give the court powers to manage cases. There is an emphasis in the CPR on:

o   'proportionality' – avoidance of using a sledgehammer to crack a nut;

o   keeping costs under control;

o   encouraging *litigants* to act reasonably (for example, taking steps to avoid going to court in the first place);

o   encouraging them to co-operate (for example, by sharing information) if going to court is unavoidable.

Failure to comply with the spirit or letter of the rules can lead to penalties.

The CPR came into force in 1999, and they are updated regularly. There is an online version on the Department for Constitutional Affairs website. Aficionados can buy the *Civil Court Practice*, otherwise known as the *Green Book*, which includes the rules as well as other useful information.

claimant (formerly *plaintiff*) – in court proceedings, the person doing the suing.

claim form – in court proceedings, an official form setting out what the claimant wants.

counterclaim – in court proceedings, a claim by the defendant against the claimant. A counterclaim is not the same as a defence, but often operates as if it were.

county court – the local court for non-criminal claims.

Debt claims under £15,000 must be started in your local *county court* (as opposed to the *High Court*). If the debt claim is £15,000 or more, you can start it in the county court, or the High Court if you wish (see Chapter 3).

creditor – a person or organisation to whom money is owed.

'Credit' and 'creditor' both come from *credo*, which is Latin for 'believe or trust' – as in the Church of England creed ('I believe in one God ...'). When you buy something on credit, the supplier lets you have it in the belief that you will pay for it, so a creditor is somebody who has supplied you with goods or money in the belief that you will pay what you owe.

company voluntary arrangement (CVA) – a private deal between a company and its creditors for repayment of debts, supervised by a *licensed insolvency practitioner*.

debtor – a person or organisation that owes, ie is in debt to, a **creditor**.

default judgment – a legal walkover, where the other side either does not reply to a *claim* or does not defend the whole or part of it.

defendant – in court proceedings, the person being sued.

enforcement – in court proceedings, the legal process by which the claimant enforces payment of a *judgment debt*.

ex parte – a 'one-sided' hearing in the absence of one party (see p 69). An ordinary hearing, with both parties present, is *inter partes*. This is a piece of law-speak which has so far defied modernisation because all lawyers understand what it means and there is really no concise English equivalent.

fast track – in the county court, the normal track (see *track*, below) for claims of more than £5,000 and not exceeding £15,000.

High Court – the court which may be appropriate for high-value and/or complex debt claims. Debt claims under £15,000 cannot be started in the High Court. You can say 'the High Court' to mean either a District Registry (attached to a *county court*) or the Royal Courts of Justice in London.

income payments order – an order from a court for a proportion of a *bankrupt*'s income to be paid to his *Trustee in Bankruptcy*, ultimately for the benefit of the creditors.

instalment order – an order by the court for a debt to be repaid by instalments.

issue – in court proceedings, to put the court's official stamp on your claim form.

individual voluntary arrangement (IVA) – a private deal for the repayment of debts between an individual debtor and their creditors, supervised by a *licensed insolvency practitioner* (the equivalent for companies is a *CVA* – see above).

judgment – a decision by a court about the merits of a claim. *Note that having a judgment against someone does **not** guarantee you will get your money.*

judgment debt – a debt for which you have a court judgment in your favour, enabling you, if the money is not immediately forthcoming, to go on to the next stage – *enforcement*.

Letter of Claim – a letter to your debtor (see 'Sample letters') warning them of your intention to start legal proceedings if they do not pay up.

Before suing anyone, the courts expect you to:

o   explain to the debtor what you want them to pay, and why;
o   make a genuine effort to recover your money;
o   give the debtor a final warning.

This is in the spirit of the *CPR*. Follow our sequence of letters – reminder, yellow card, red card, etc (see 'Sample letters'). If you do not at least send a Letter of Claim the judge can penalise you, regardless of whether you win or lose.

---

licensed insolvency practitioner – a professional, usually an accountant or a lawyer, who is qualified to take over the financial affairs of someone who is *bankrupt*, or a company in *liquidation*.

liquidation – similar to *bankruptcy*, except this is for companies and not for individuals. Also known as *winding-up*.

The main difference is that the company debtor's slate is wiped clean only if and when it has paid its debts in full (a rare event).

litigation – legal proceedings.

litigant – someone involved in *litigation*.

litigant in person – a *litigant* who is not represented by a lawyer (a litigious person is someone with a taste for litigation, who sues people at the drop of a hat).

multi-track – in the county court, the normal *track* (see *track* below) for claims of £15,000 or more.

official receiver (OR) – the government officer who takes over a *bankrupt*'s financial affairs in the first instance when a *bankruptcy* order is made; the OR may subsequently be replaced by a *licensed insolvency practitioner*.

order to obtain information – formerly known as *oral examination*: a question and answer session in court to find out about a debtor's financial situation.

You can't have an order to obtain information until you have a *judgment debt*. The order doesn't get you the money there and then, but it may give you the information you need to decide what method of *enforcement* to try (see Chapter 8).

personal service – the delivery by hand of an important document by leaving it with the recipient (rather than using post, fax, email, etc) because that is what the law requires. You can always *choose* to deliver a document by personal service. Although it is sometimes compulsory, personal service is the exception rather than the rule. We will alert you when personal service is required.

Personal service can be tricky if the debtor is keeping out of the way.

To 'effect personal service on' (law-speak for deliver by hand to) an individual, you must put the document into their hands or, if they will not accept it, lay it at their feet. You should also always tell the recipient what the document is, particularly if it is in an envelope.

To effect personal service on a company, do the same and get the document into the hands (or at the feet) of a director or company secretary. Leaving it at the reception desk won't do!

If in doubt, pay a *process server* to do the deed.

petition – in certain proceedings, including *bankruptcy*, an application to the court.

preferential debts – in the context of *bankruptcy/liquidation* proceedings, debts which get paid before other unsecured debts.

Examples of preferential debts are pension contributions and employees' wages. The fees of the *licensed insolvency practitioner* looking after a *bankrupt*'s financial affairs are not a debt but a charge on the assets, and these are paid before anything or anyone else.

process server – someone who **serves** official documents and provides proof that they have done so.

Register of County Court Judgments – an official list of *judgment debts* which were not paid promptly. The list does not include:

o judgment debts which were paid within 28 days of the date of judgment;

o judgment debts which are more than six years old;

o judgment debts where judgment was given in the High Court.

secured creditor – a *creditor*, for example a mortgage lender, with rights over specific assets of the **debtor** for the purpose of compelling payment. Such rights enable the creditor to sell the assets if the debtor defaults. The opposite is, of course, an *unsecured creditor*, who has no such rights.

service – the legal term for *sending or handing over* an important document. Unless there is a requirement for *personal service* (see above), first-class post is sufficient. Do not use fax unless the other side agrees, and do not use email unless the other side has solicitors and they agree to email being used. All the same, a fax or email followed by the original by first-class post has a certain 'shock and awe' value. Do not use 'recorded delivery' – in our experience, a sneaky debtor will smell a rat and refuse to accept the item.

set aside – law-speak for 'cancel' (as in 'set aside a claim') rather than an agreement to pay a farmer a fortune to grow thistles on their land!

small claims track – in the context of debt recovery in the county court, the track (see *track* below) which deals with debt claims with a financial value not exceeding £5,000.

The procedures on the small claims track are less formal than on the other tracks, so that creditors with small claims can conduct their own cases without legal representation as *litigants in person*.

statutory demand – a formal demand for payment of a debt, as the first stage of *bankruptcy* or *liquidation* proceedings.

A statutory demand must be made on the official form and *personal service* on the debtor, if an individual, is obligatory (see p 81).

summary judgment – in court proceedings, a quickie judgment available where the debtor tells the court they will defend, but it is obvious to the court that they have 'no real prospect of succeeding'.

third party debt order (formerly known, much more interestingly, as a *garnishee order*) – a court order for a debtor's money in a bank or building society account to be paid direct to a *claimant* to pay a *judgment debt* (see p 67).

track – in the county court, defended claims are assigned to one of three 'tracks', or sets of procedures, according to their value and complexity.

These are the *small claims track*, the *fast track* and the *multi-track*. Small claims track procedures are simpler than the fast track, and so on.

Trustee in Bankruptcy (TiB) – the person who administers and realises the assets of a *bankrupt* and distributes the proceeds for the benefit of the bankrupt's *creditors*.

warrant of execution – an authority given by the court for the *bailiffs* to swing into action.

wind up – to put a company into *liquidation*.

Frequently asked questions (FAQs)

Can I go to court if I can't afford the court fees?

Yes. You may not have to pay any court fees if you receive:

o   income support;

o   working tax credit/child tax credit;

o   disability working allowance;

o   jobseeker's allowance; *or if*

o   paying the court fee would cause you financial hardship.

There is a special form, EX160, to complete if you think you qualify. There is also a leaflet, EX160A: *Court Fees – Do You Have To Pay Them?* (both the form and the leaflet are available from any court, or from the Court Service website – click on 'Forms and guidance').

Can it be cost effective to get a debt collection agency or a solicitor to collect my debts for me?

The answer is a definite maybe.

If you engage a debt collection agency, you will not be able to claim their charges from the debtor unless your contract with the debtor gives you the right to do so. In any case, they will usually only threaten and cajole: they are not lawyers and will not normally go to court for you.

If you engage a solicitor to recover a debt of under £5,000, your court claim can include only a modest fixed amount for the solicitor's charges, which is unlikely to cover what you pay out. The small claims track is geared to doing it yourself, but it may still be worth your while to get a professional to recover the debt for you depending, for example, on how much a professional will charge and the value you put on your own time.

Can I 'send the boys round'?

No. Harassment of debtors is a criminal offence under the Administration of Justice Act 1970. Harassment is not limited to violence or the threat of violence – it can include threats of publicity and demands that, by reason of their frequency or aggressive content, are designed to alarm or humiliate the debtor. On the other hand, in 2001 the Court of Appeal in *Thomas v News Group Newspapers* decided that 'Press criticism, even if robust, does not fall within the natural meaning of harassment'. So when you shop your debtor to the *News of the World*, remember to quote *Thomas v News Group Newspapers* and you should be OK. However, breaking the debtor's windows is out of line and is, indeed, criminal damage.

You can make a personal visit to the debtor, but *be polite*. There are also special rules for residential landlords, who must not harass their tenants.

Is non-payment of debts a criminal offence?

No, not usually, and it *is* a criminal offence to try to extract payment by suggesting that it is.

However, a debtor who systematically bounces cheques in order to obtain goods and/or services may be committing a criminal offence. In a case like this you could contact the police, who may or may not decide to become involved. Remember, though, that calling the cops does not usually bring *you* any closer to getting your money.

Can I take the goods back if they're not paid for?

Only in exceptional cases:

o where your contract of sale says that the goods belong to you until they are fully paid for; *and*

o where the goods remain separate from the debtor's other property and belongings (so you could take back a television but not a central heating system); *and*

o where the debtor gives you permission to take the goods back (you can't force entry onto the debtor's premises), *or* you obtain a court order to do so.

Remember, of course, that if you do take the goods back, they are now second-hand and cannot be re-sold as new.

I have repaired the debtor's car. Can I hold onto it until I am paid?

The good news is 'yes, you can'. Also, if the debtor still doesn't pay up you can ultimately get a court order for the **bailiffs** to sell the car at auction and use the net proceeds towards the debt.

The bad news is, it isn't as simple as that. *The bailiffs* do the selling, not you. That is because you do not own the car, so it is not yours to sell. Also, of course, it may be subject to a finance arrangement, which probably means that whoever sells the car, the finance house will take its money and leave very little for you.

I am half way through re-roofing a customer's house. The customer won't make interim payments. Can I come off the job until I get some money?

No. Unless your contract gives you a specific right to interim payments, you have to complete the job before you can demand payment.

Do I have to wait before I can sue?

Not always. You have to wait for the period of time which your contract allows for payment (often, for example, 28 days). If your contract entitles you to 'payment on demand', you can in theory sue as soon as you send your invoice.

Warning: be reasonable

Remember the **Civil Procedure Rules (CPR)**. Even if you win your case, the court may disallow your costs if your conduct has been unreasonable – for example, if you have not given the customer written warning (often called a **Letter of Claim**) of your intention to take them to court.

Do I have to wait before starting bankruptcy proceedings?

No, but the debt must be due and payable immediately. Also, remember, there is a waiting period built into the procedure – the debtor has 21 days to respond to your **statutory demand**.

Can I claim interest on the original debt?

Yes – see 'Interest', p 24.

Can I claim interest on a judgment debt?

Yes, but only if:

o   the judgment debt is for not less than £5,000; *or*

o   it is one to which the Late Payment of Commercial Debts (Interest) Act 1998 applies (see p 25).

Can I claim for my own time/my firm's time in collecting the debt?

No, sorry – not unless your contract with the debtor gives you the right to do so.

What you can do, however, is claim compensation for late payment where the debtor is another business (it doesn't work for private consumers). There are fixed rates for compensation on a sliding scale:

Amount of debt (excluding interest) £	Compensation £
Up to 999.99	40
1,000 to 9,999.99	70
10,000 or more	100

Not very generous, but every little helps.

Can I offer incentives for early payment?

Yes. A small discount, perhaps, or a free tea towel – the choice is yours!

I have a judgment debt. Can I pursue more than one method of enforcement at the same time?

The general rule is 'yes', but there are exceptions. The main exception is that you cannot, unless the court agrees otherwise, pursue other methods if you already have an **attachment of earnings** order.

Remember that an **order to obtain information** *is not a method of enforcement*, so you can resort to this at any time and it may help you decide how far along the road to pursue your debtor.

Spotting a doubtful customer

You are unlikely to want to supply goods or services – or indeed to lend money – to a person who is unwilling or unable to pay you. The best way of avoiding bad debts is to pick your customers with care. If you have serious doubts about a person's willingness or ability to pay, you can check them out.

Much financial information about people is confidential, and is protected by the Data Protection Act 1998. There are, however, sources of information which are publicly accessible.

o   *The Register of County Court Judgments* (see 'Useful contacts') is maintained by the Registry Trust Limited. For £4.50 per name (make out the cheque to Registry Trust Limited) you can get a print-out of any judgments against that name. You can also download an application form from the Registry Trust website, complete the form on-screen, print it and mail it.

Note that this register does not include High Court judgments (which do not figure on any register), so really big debts can go unrecorded.

---

o   *The Individual Insolvency Register*, which came into operation in March 1999, keeps details of **bankruptcy** and **individual voluntary arrangements** (**IVAs**). You can apply free of charge

- *in person* at any official receiver's office (listed in your local telephone directory), where you fill in a form and receive a print-out of the information;
- *in writing* to the Insolvency Service;
- *by telephone* to the Insolvency Service, and they will tell you over the telephone whether an *individual* is **bankrupt** or is subject to bankruptcy proceedings or has entered into an IVA.

o The *Insolvency Service helpline* will also tell you whether a *company* has gone into compulsory **liquidation** or is subject to liquidation proceedings, or has entered into a **company voluntary arrangement (CVA)**. There is no charge.

The *Insolvency Service Disqualified Directors Hotline* was set up 'to catch defiant directors and undischarged bankrupts who blatantly disregard disqualification orders made against them'. It is open 24 hours a day and will tell you free of charge whether someone is on their list of people who are disqualified from acting as company directors.

o You can also seek information from a licensed credit reference agency, most of which use 'credit scoring systems' and then allocate a pass mark to predict whether or not people are a good credit risk. See the Yellow Pages for your local agencies, or call Talking Pages (see 'Useful contacts') for a free nationwide trawl.

Using a credit reference agency will, of course, cost you money and may not be totally reliable.

If you are seriously doubtful about someone's ability to pay and you don't mind being unpopular, you can ask them to show to your satisfaction where they will get the money – or else insist on money up front.

Prevention is better than cure

If you *must* deal with potentially unreliable customers:

o   ask for payment in cleared funds (cash, credit card, electronic transfer, bank draft or building society equivalent) in advance, or on delivery;

o   hold on to the goods or the customer's property (for example, the lawnmower which they have handed over to you for repairing) until you are paid;

o   ask for, and obtain, security – such as a signed guarantee;

o   think carefully about your standard terms and conditions of trade. For example, if you supply goods, do the goods remain yours until they are fully paid for? If you provide a service, are you entitled to instalments?

2

Where do I start?

Most debt recovery is a matter of organisation, persistence and good communication. Remember: *going to court is always a last resort, and involves irrecoverable time and expense.*

Here are the first stages on the road to debt recovery. To make things clearer, we have set this out in a flowchart on pp 8–9.

○ **invoice the customer**

Make sure the invoice is consistent with your contract. It is helpful if the invoice re-states the contractual period for payment (such as 28 days) and, if applicable, reminds the customer that you can charge interest. Consider also putting on the invoice a note on what the customer should do if they are unable to pay immediately (such as letting you know at once).

○ **first reminder**

We give a sample letter on p 112.

○ **stiff letter** – the 'yellow warning'. See our sample letter on p 113.

○ **ring the debtor** – be polite, be firm and *keep a careful note for your file of what is said and agreed.* You may think you'll remember what was said, but we guarantee that in a week's time your memory will be as hazy as anyone else's. On-the-spot notes, which professionals call 'file notes' or 'attendance notes', are an invaluable record and could help you win your case. Try to find out why you are not being paid and do a deal if you can – for example, for payment by instalments (with interest, if chargeable, on the late money). If appropriate, follow up the call with another letter confirming what was said. We give a sample letter on p 115 which summarises the debtor's proposals for payment.

- **final warning** – the 'red card'! We give a sample **Letter of Claim** on p 114.

- **ongoing enquiries** – from the beginning, try to find out what you can from the debtor about their financial circumstances, such as ownership of property, savings, employment and, of course, other debts. Keep good file notes of this information – you may well need them.

Decision time

You have issued your final warning and you still haven't been paid. You need to know why.

Can't pay?

You can't get blood out of a stone. If your debtor is genuinely unable to pay, consider whether any further action would involve throwing good money after bad.

In particular, do not waste time and money taking court proceedings against

- an individual without checking on the Individual Insolvency Register (see p 1) whether they are already bankrupt, or
- a company without checking with the Insolvency Service (see p 2) whether the company has already gone into liquidation.

In either situation, you could sue them and get your judgment, but the court can make you apply to set the judgment aside (cancel it) – at *your* expense!

But people's financial circumstances can change, so:

- keep the file open;
- ask the debtor to provide a *statement of means* (see the sample on p 123);

o　　try to persuade the debtor to pay at least nominal instalments;

o　　review the case periodically in case the debtor comes into money;

o　　keep an eye on the time limit for court proceedings. You can't sue on a contract debt more than six years after the date of the contract.

Can pay, won't pay?

There are two possibilities here. We have all met people who are quick to order goods and services but slow to pay for them, and it may be your misfortune to be dealing with one of them.

The second possibility is that the person is withholding payment for a good reason. Do they have a genuine cause for complaint or dispute? If so, you will make the task of collecting the debt a lot easier if you resolve the dispute before you go to court. What's more, it may well be that with the dispute out of the way you will get paid in any case. Consider whether your standard terms and conditions of business should include a complaints procedure.

Debt recover: the early stages

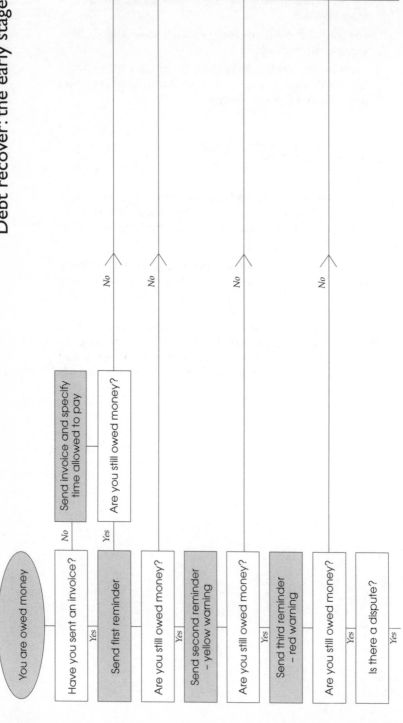

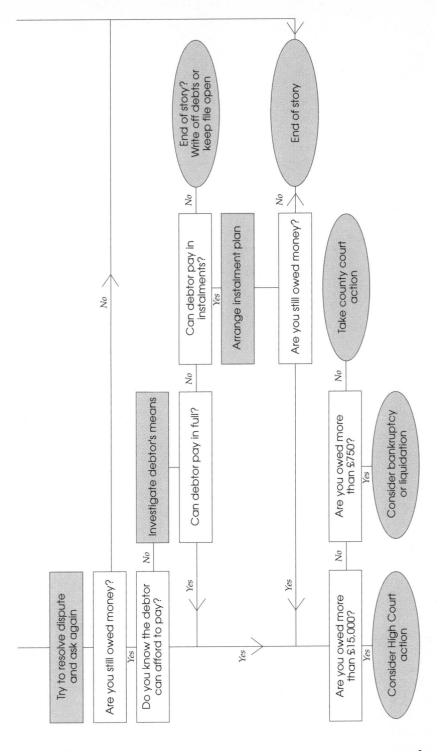

3

Choosing your weapon

If you have security over any of your debtor's assets, now is the time to get your money by realising the security. You may still need a court order to do this – take legal advice.

Otherwise, you have two choices:

o   **bankruptcy/liquidation** proceedings, or
o   court proceedings for recovery of the debt.

Let's consider bankruptcy or liquidation first. Insolvency cramps everyone's style, and members of some professions are actually barred from practising if they are insolvent. The threat of bankruptcy (for an individual) or liquidation (for a company) may therefore concentrate your debtor's mind wonderfully, and you can do the threatening free of charge with a **statutory demand** (see Chapter 14), but remember:

o   **bankruptcy** proceedings are limited to debts of £750 or more, and the same limit (with exceptions) applies to **liquidation** proceedings;
o   bankruptcy/liquidation proceedings are not suitable where the court might find that the debtor has genuine grounds for disputing your claim;
o   the threat – particularly the statutory demand – is often more potent than the deed itself.

This is because taking bankruptcy/liquidation proceedings does not get you to the front of the queue of creditors.

If you have security of some kind, such as bricks and mortar, you may be lucky because creditors with valid security can realise the secured assets to get their money (see p xx). All creditors – including **secured creditors** to the extent that there is a shortfall in their security that they want to make up out of the communal pot – can claim in the bankruptcy/liquidation, but they all have to join the queue.

First in line are the **licensed insolvency practitioners**, whose fees count as a charge against the bankrupt's assets.

Next come any **preferential debts**. These are paid in full before other creditors are even considered.

Then, what's left is shared out and all such 'other creditors' are paid proportionately according to the value of their claims – one penny in the pound is not unusual. So, if you bankrupt somebody you may end up going to a great deal of expense and doing a lot of work for someone else's benefit, including the debtor's.

Compared with taking action in the county court, bankruptcy/liquidation is expensive.

The court fee for a creditor's bankruptcy petition is £180. You also have to make an advance payment to the Insolvency Service of £300, although in theory this may be refundable if the bankrupt's assets allow. For liquidation of a limited company, the court fee is £180 and the Insolvency Service fee is £500.

The county court

This option will be appropriate:

o   where the debt is less than £15,000, for which you cannot use the High Court. In practice, a debt claim with a value of less than £50,000 should be started in the county court, since if it is defended the High Court will transfer it to the county court anyway;

o   where the debt is disputed;

o   where the high costs of bankruptcy/liquidation deter you and/or the debtor's financial situation means that you will not get your money by that route. Note also that if the debt is less than £750, the option of bankruptcy/liquidation is in any case not open to you (see above);

o   where you can see your way clear to **enforcing** your court judgment. There are various means open to you:

- where the debtor is in employment, consider getting an **attachment of earnings order**;
- where the debtor has valuable belongings, consider calling in the **bailiffs**;
- where the debtor has savings, consider a **third party debt order**;
- where the debtor owns their own home or other bricks and mortar, consider a **charging order**.

We will tell you how to go about all of these in Chapter 8.

The High Court

A High Court action (normally outside the scope of this book) will be appropriate:

o   where the debt is of high value (minimum £15,000) and the case is complex;

o   where you want to use High Court **enforcement** procedures – see below on **judgment debts** over £5,000.

One option to bear in mind is to *start* proceedings in the county court and *transfer* them to the High Court for enforcement. You *must* transfer if you want a judgment debt of over £5,000 enforced by seizure and sale of goods. You may also be able to get interest in the High Court where it is not available in the county court.

In practice, if you as an individual want to use the High Court, you should take legal advice. Companies cannot use the High Court unless they are represented by a solicitor.

County court action

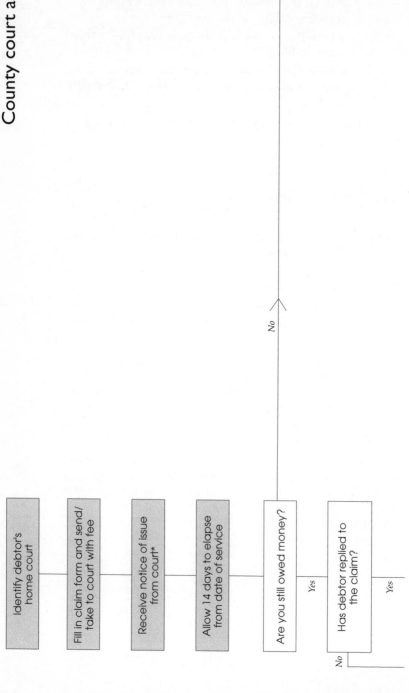

Identify debtor's home court

Fill in claim form and send/take to court with fee

Receive notice of issue from court*

Allow 14 days to elapse from date of service

Are you still owed money? — No

Yes

Has debtor replied to the claim?

Yes

No

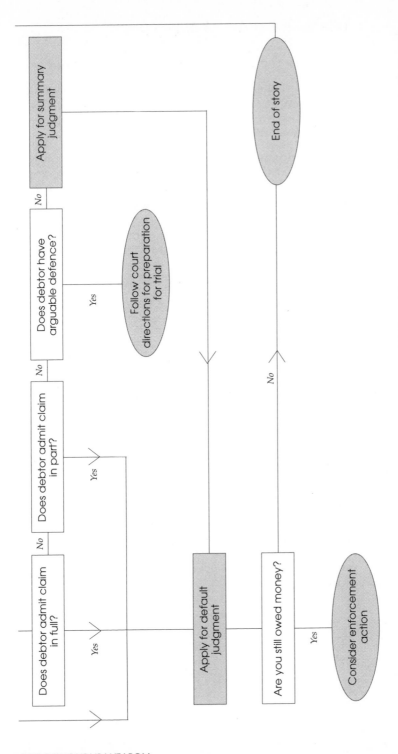

* Alternatively, to save time, you can serve the claim form yourself, but before doing so you must still send it to the court with the fee

Taking the county court option

See you in the county court – but which one?

Which court should you use? You can start proceedings in any county court. You may think that your own local court is the most convenient for you, but this isn't necessarily so.

If the debtor is an individual (that is, not a limited company), it is often more far-sighted to start proceedings in the court *nearest to where the debtor lives* (in other words, the debtor's 'home' court). This is because claims defended by individuals are automatically transferred to the debtor's 'home' court, and **orders to obtain information** (see below) and most **enforcement** procedures have to be carried out there too, however inconvenient this is for you.

If you do not know which is the debtor's 'home' court, your own local county court can tell you.

You may have to apply to transfer your case to the debtor's 'home' court if:

o   the debtor moves house; or

o   you want to submit the debtor to an **order to obtain information**; or

o   you want to **enforce** your **judgment**.

You make the application by written request to the court, quoting the case number. There is no special form. Just use the sample letter on p 116.

If the debtor is a company, its 'home' court is the one nearest its principal place of business. Defended claims against companies are not automatically transferred to the company's 'home' court, but for enforcement purposes the 'home' court is often the best place to start proceedings.

The nitty gritty: filling in the claim form

The first thing to do is to fill in N1, the claim form. A blank version is reproduced here, and you will find a worked example on p 118. You can obtain form N1 as well as form N1A (Notes for Claimant) from any court, or download them from the Court Service website.

The other way of filing your claim is to use the Court Service's Money Claim Online facilities. We describe the procedure in detail on p 31. Meanwhile, back to the paper claim form.

The notes that accompany the claim form are clear and helpful, but they cover all types of claims. In our notes below we concentrate on claims for debt.

Claim Form

In the

for court use only

Claim No.	
Issue date	

Claimant

SEAL

Defendant(s)

Brief details of claim

Value

Defendant's name and address			£
	Amount claimed		
	Court fee		
	Solicitor's costs		
	Total amount		

The court office at

is open between 10 am and 4 pm Monday to Friday. When corresponding with the court, please address forms or letters to the Court Manager and quote the claim number.
N1 Claim form (CPR Part 7) (01.02)

Printed on behalf of The Court Service

	Claim No.	

Does, or will, your claim include any issues under the Human Rights Act 1998? ☐ Yes ☐ No

Particulars of Claim (attached)(to follow)

Statement of Truth
*(I believe)(The Claimant believes) that the facts stated in these particulars of claim are true.
* I am duly authorised by the claimant to sign this statement

Full name _____

Name of claimant's solicitor's firm _____

signed _____ position or office held _____
*(Claimant)(Litigation friend)(Claimant's solicitor) (if signing on behalf of firm or company)
*delete as appropriate

	Claimant's or claimant's solicitor's address to which documents or payments should be sent if different from overleaf including (if appropriate) details of DX, fax or e-mail.

1 In the ...

The name of the court should include the words 'County Court' – for example, Eatanswill County Court.

2 Claim No

Do not fill in the claim number box – the court will allocate a number to your case and fill in this box for you.

3 Issue date

The court will complete the issue date.

4 Claimant

You are the *claimant*, and this is where you fill in *your name and address.*

o   If you are a sole trader, and use another name for your business, write in your own name, then the words 'trading as' followed by your trade name.

o   If you are a firm (two or more people in business together), write in the firm name followed by the words 'a firm'.

o   If you are a limited company, write in the name of the company including the word 'Limited'.

Insert your business address, and include postcode, telephone number, fax number and email address if you have one.

If you are under the age of 18 you will need an adult – for example, a parent – to help you with your claim. The adult is called your litigation friend. After your name, add 'suing by his/her *litigation friend*' and insert your litigation friend's name. The litigation friend has to fill in another court form (not provided in this book but obtainable from the court), promising to pay any money that the court may order you to pay to the debtor in the course of the proceedings (for example, costs).

5 Defendant(s)

On the claim form the debtor is referred to as the *defendant*. This is where you put the *debtor's name and address*. Take great care to get their name right.

o   If the debtor is an individual, specify Mr/Mrs/ Miss/Ms etc, as appropriate, provide first names if you know them or initials otherwise, and surname.

o   If the debtor is a sole trader and uses another name for their business, write in their own name, then the words 'trading as' followed by their trade name.

o   If the debtor is a firm (two or more people in business together), write in the firm name followed by the words 'a firm'.

o   If the debtor is a limited company, give the name of the company and the company registration number. You can get this number by doing a free search at Companies House either by telephone (general enquiries) or on their website.

While the company number is not obligatory, bear in mind that every company number is unique (like a car registration number or your National Insurance number) and, in a case where several companies have very similar names, quoting the company number could avoid any confusion.

o   Insert the debtor's address, preferably including the postcode:

–   for a private individual, use the debtor's home address;

–   for a business debtor, use their principal place of business.

If the address is outside England and Wales, take professional advice.

The Lord Chancellor's White Paper (March 2003), snappily entitled *Effective Enforcement: Improved Methods of Recovery for Civil Court Debt and Commercial Rent and a Single Regulatory Regime for Warrant Enforcement Agents*, noted that 50% of all bailiffs' warrants were unenforceable because they were incorrectly addressed. This begs the question of whether the original claims were wrong too! There is no point in getting a judgment against a debtor who never receives the claim form because they can have it **set aside**. So do your homework before you file your claim. You can read the White Paper yourself at www.dca.gov.uk/enforcement/wp.

6 Brief details of claim

You can keep this short and simple. Just make it clear that the claim is for payment of money for supply of goods or services or, for example, for repayment of a loan.

7 Value

Insert the amount of your claim here, *excluding* interest and court fees. (The amount you claim in box 9 will include the interest. The court fee goes in at box 10.)

8 Defendant's name and address

There is another box at the bottom of the claim form for the defendant's name and address.

o   If you are suing one person only, repeat the name and address of the defendant in this box.

o   If you are suing more than one person, you will need a separate form for each defendant. Put in the names of *all* the defendants at the top of each form, and use the box at the bottom of each form to give the name and address of *each* defendant separately. You will need to repeat all the information about the particulars of the claim *on each form*.

9 Amount claimed

Insert the value of your claim *plus interest at the date of issue of proceedings.*

10 Court fee

The court fee at the time of writing is on a sliding scale according to value as follows:

Amount claimed not more than £	Fee £
300	30
500	50
1,000	80
5,000	120
15,000	250
50,000	400

You can check the current fee either by calling your court or checking on the Court Service website – click on 'county court fees'.

11 Solicitor's costs

If you are a **litigant in person** – that is, acting for yourself – you cannot claim solicitor's costs. Put N/A here.

12 Total amount

This is the amount you are claiming, plus the court fee.

First tick the NO box next to 'Does, or will, your claim include any issues under the Human Rights Act 1998?'

Now tell the court how the debt arose.

Keep it brief – unless you anticipate that the claim will be defended, in which case you need to get your story in first! Give brief details of the contract terms:

o   the date of contract;

o   the type of contract (whether written or oral);

o   the nature of goods or services provided;

o   the price;

o   other relevant terms, such as time allowed for payment.

You should also provide the invoice number, the date, the invoice amount, the amount of any payments made and the balance outstanding.

See our worked example on p 119.

Where the contract is written, you should attach a copy of the contract. In any event, attach a copy of your invoice.

However blindingly obvious the merits of your case may seem to you, a judge will expect evidence to back up your claim. The term *burden of proof (onus probandi)* is probably familiar to you. In a legal context it means the responsibility of a claimant to provide evidence in support of a claim. So make sure you provide it!

Interest

You won't get interest unless you claim it. There are three possibilities. You must decide which applies to you. Each is governed by a different set of rules and the interests rates vary too.

1   **Contractual interest** – if your contract with the debtor gives you the right to this. Check your contract to see exactly what interest rate it says you can claim, although note that grossly unfair terms and conditions can be challenged (see 'Contractual interest', below).

2 **Statutory interest on commercial debt** – if both you and your debtor are in business, you have a right under the Late Payment of Commercial Debts (Interest) Act 1998. On sales after 7 August 2002, interest can be claimed on all business-to-business debt. For sales before that date, this claim can only be made by small businesses (50 or fewer employees) (see 'Statutory claim', below).

3 **Discretionary interest** – if neither 1 nor 2 applies, you can still ask the court to award interest at its discretion under the County Courts Act 1984 (see 'Discretionary interest', below).

○ Do interest calculations make your brain hurt? Go to www.payontime.co.uk for a handy interest calculator. This site also has useful guidance on statutory interest on commercial debt and other goodies, such as credit management advice.

○ You will not be awarded two lots of interest on the same amount. Where your claim is under the 1998 or 1984 Acts (see above), you will not be awarded **compound interest**.

1 Contractual interest

The interest rate

This will be whatever your contract entitles you to.

The wording on the claim form

The claimant has a contractual right to interest.

Interest is claimed from: *[insert date from which interest runs, for example, 28 days from date of invoice, if that is what your contract specifies]*

Interest is claimed to: *[insert date – which must not be after the date of issue of the claim form]*

Interest is claimed on: *[insert amount of debt, before interest]*

Total interest to the date of calculation is: *[insert amount]*

The daily rate of interest after the date of calculation is: *[insert daily rate].*

2 Statutory claim – Late Payment of Commercial Debts (Interest) Act 1998

The interest rate

This will be 8% above what is known as the 'reference rate', which at the time of writing is 4%. To find out the current reference rate and to calculate the interest quickly, go to the interest calculator at www.payontime.co.uk.

The wording on the claim form

> The claimant claims interest under the Late Payment of Commercial Debts (Interest) Act 1998 at the rate of *[insert rate]* from *[insert date from which interest runs, for example, 28 days from date of invoice]*. Interest is claimed to: *[insert date – which must not be after the date of issue of the claim form]* in the sum of *[insert amount]* and continuing at the same rate up to the date of judgment, or earlier payment, at the daily rate of *[enter daily rate of interest]*.

3 Discretionary claim – County Courts Act 1984

The interest rate

8% simple per annum.

The wording on the claim form

> The claimant claims interest under section 69 of the County Courts Act 1984 at the rate of 8% a year, from *[date when the money became owed to you]* to *[the date when you are issuing the claim]* of £ *[put in the amount]* and also interest at the same rate up to the date of judgment, or earlier payment, at a daily rate of *[enter the daily rate of interest]*.

Calculating the daily rate of interest

If you are not into DIY interest calculations, go to www.payontime.co.uk which will give you a daily rate on statutory interest. Otherwise, using your calculator:

o   enter the amount of the debt;

o   multiply by the interest rate;

o   press the % button;

o   divide by 365.

This gets you the daily rate.

For the interest you are owed to date, multiply the daily rate by the number of days the debt has remained unpaid.

Compensation

You can also claim compensation for late payment where the debtor is another business (sorry, it doesn't work for private consumers). There are fixed rates for compensation on a sliding scale:

Amount of debt (excluding interest) £	Compensation £
Up to 999.99	40
1,000 to 9,999.99	70
10,000 or more	100

Not very generous, but every little helps. The wording to add to the claim form is:

> The claimant claims compensation arising from late payment under section 5a Late Payment of Commercial Debts (Interest) Act 1998. Under the table of compensation set out in this provision, £ *[insert amount of compensation]* is owed.

14 Statement of Truth

This allows the facts set out in the 'Particulars of Claim' to be treated as evidence. The person signing the statement should write in their name clearly and sign. If you are a limited company, the Statement of Truth should be signed by a director, company secretary or manager, and the signatory's position in the company should be stated.

15 Claimant's or claimant's solicitor's address

This address box is meant for claimants' solicitors. You do not need to use this box as long as your address on the front of the form is the one you want the court to use.

Now what?

Take or post to the court:

o   one copy of the claim form for the court plus one copy for each defendant;

o   the court fee.

You can pay in cash (in which case, use registered post or deliver personally), or by cheque made out to HMPG (Her Majesty's Paymaster General).

Keep a copy of the claim form(s) for your file.

The court will now – provided you got your form-filling right – **issue** your claim form (put an official stamp on it) and **serve** it on the debtor.

Service

The court normally posts the issued claim form to the defendant. At the same time, the court sends you a form called *Notice of Issue (Specified Amount) and Request for Judgment* (see 'Getting a **default judgment**', p 38). You cannot get this form from the Court Service website. The form tells you the date of **service**, that is, the date on which, according to the court rules, the debtor is deemed to have received the claim form. According to the court, first-class post takes two days. If the court posts the claim form, the date of service is *two days after posting*.

You may be able to speed up the procedure if you are prepared to serve the issued claim form yourself, *but*:

o   a tricky defendant may deny ever receiving the claim form; and

o   within seven days after the date of service you *must* notify the court of the date and method of service, using form N215, available on the Court Service website or from your local court. *If you do not send form N215 to the court you cannot get judgment.*

If you want to serve the claim form yourself, collect the defendant's copy of the issued claim form from the court, or ask them to send it back to you.

You can **serve** it by:

o   delivery to the defendant's address. **Personal service** is not necessary; it is sufficient to put the claim form through the debtor's letterbox. Make a note of the day you delivered the claim form. The date of service, according to court rules, will be the *day after you delivered the claim form.*

o   fax – in which case, keep your transmission sheet as well as the fax itself;

o   email – in which case, print out a copy from your Sent Mail box and keep it on file.

Claiming online

If you are confident about using the internet to book flights and order flowers, you may prefer to make your claim online at Money Claim Online (MCOL). At least you won't have to provide multiple copies or trek down to the post office with your forms. Type www.courtservice.gov.uk/mcol or click on the link from the website accompanying this book.

The Court Service describes MCOL as 'a simple, convenient and secure way of making or responding to a money claim on the internet'. It is supported by a customer helpdesk and a tutorial service.

Start by clicking in the 'I am a claimant' box. You will then have to log in as a new customer, giving a user name and a password.

Before you can proceed, the site advises: 'If you have any doubt as to the viability or validity of your case we would advise you to seek independent legal advice before proceeding. Remember you may be liable for your opponent's costs in the event of your action being unsuccessful.' In other words, don't go ahead with this unless you are sure you are in the right! We couldn't have put it better ourselves.

The Money Claim Online website lists people who cannot use the service. These include Vexatious Litigants and people under the age of 18. Fair enough – but they also say, 'Examples of who cannot be sued online are

o   Government
o   The Monarchy'

so if you were thinking of using MCOL to sue the Inland Revenue or the Queen, tough ...

Everything you type in is automatically saved online. You can also save your completed forms to your computer and print hard copies for your paper file.

The printed copies are for your own reference only. They cannot be accepted by a county court; if you want to take that route you will have to fill in an ordinary paper form N1.

You are advised to check that MCOL is suitable for your claim:

o   your claim must be for a fixed amount of money (up to £99,999.99);

o   it must be against not more than two defendants;

o   you must have an address in England or Wales where documents can be delivered;

o   all defendants must have an address in England or Wales where documents can be delivered;

o   you must have an email address.

If you can't answer 'Yes' to all these points, you are advised to go to the Customer Help Desk for advice.

Now for the form-filling

As you would expect, you will have to provide your own name and address and the name and address of the defendant(s). That should be simple but, like many online facilities, this one is pedantic. Rosy tested the system by filing a sample claim against Mark Fairweather's firm, Fairweather Stephenson & Co, only to have the system reject the ampersand (&) sign. However, once she got to the Particulars of Claim everything went smoothly. The system even calculates the court fee for you.

There is no need for a signature; you type in your surname and initial in the signature box. The next screen confirms the parties' names and the amount of the claim and invites you to pay by credit card or debit card.

Afterwards the system sends you an email to confirm that you have registered.

Reassuringly, in case your computer turns awkward their Customer Help Desk can also be contacted by telephone. Call 0845 601 5935 between 9 am and 5 pm Monday to Friday.

6

What happens next?

Now turn to the flowchart on pp 14–15. You have **served** the claim on the debtor, or the court has done so and sent you the Notice of Issue. Whether you claimed online or through the county court, the debtor is sent a copy of your claim form and a 'response pack', which contains the forms the **defendant** can use to reply to your claim.

Knowledge is power. You will handle this matter more confidently if you know what papers the court will send to the debtor and what their options are. The debtor receives a set of *Notes For Defendant on Replying to the Claim* (form N1C) together with a response pack (N9), which contains:

o   an admission form;

o   a defence form;

o   an **acknowledgment of service**.

You can download forms N1C and N9 from the Court Service website (go to Forms and Guidance), or obtain them from your local court. Read them carefully. You will see that the debtor has the following options ...

What can the debtor do?

The debtor usually communicates with the court (not with you), although any payments they make will come direct to you. The debtor can:

1 Pay you in full

Make sure they include the court fee and any interest; give a receipt and let the court know. End of story.

2 Lie low and say nothing

The debtor must respond within the time limit that the claim form specifies, which – as long as you have filled in the Particulars of Claim on the claim form – is 14 days after the date of service (see above). Unless the debtor responds to the claim form before the deadline, you can apply for a **default judgment** – a sort of legal walkover – for the whole amount. Use the bottom part of the Notice of Issue (N205A) to request judgment.

If you have got your paperwork right, the court will send you and the defendant each a copy of form N30(1), called 'Judgment for the Claimant'.

This might seem like a great victory, but the court will not do anything to make sure you get your money unless you specifically ask them to (see Chapter 8).

Mark the deadline in your diary – and get in quick if the opportunity arises.

If the defendant does not respond, you have six months to apply for a **default judgment**. After that, your claim will be 'stayed' (that is, put on hold) and before you can proceed again you must apply to the court for permission (or *leave* in law-speak) to continue.

3 Admit the full amount of your claim, and offer to pay

The debtor does this on the Admission Form (N9A) and sends the form to *you*.

You can now ask the court to 'enter judgment on admission'. The purpose of this is – assuming that you accept the terms – to ask the court to order the debtor to pay you the amount of your claim, plus your costs, on the terms the debtor has offered. To do this, you need to fill in the bottom half of form N205A and send it to the court. There is no additional fee.

If you used MCOL, you can do this online – log onto the website and follow the instructions.

If you have got your paperwork right, the court will send you and the defendant each a copy of form N30(1): Judgment for the Claimant.

Remember that the court will not do anything to make sure you get your money unless you specifically ask them to (see Chapter 8).

What if you are not happy with the debtor's offer? Ask the court to enter judgment anyway. Fill in the bottom of form N205A, saying why you object to the terms the debtor is offering. Send or take it to the court *together with the debtor's admission form*, making sure that you have first taken copies for your own file.

A member of the court staff will decide – this is called a *determination* – how much the debtor should pay and when. The court will send you and the debtor each a form N30(2): Judgment for Claimant After Determination.

If you are still not happy with the court's determination, you have 14 days to write to the court saying why you object (there is no special form for this), sending a copy to the debtor. A judge will then decide. There is no extra fee.

The judge can decide on the basis of the paperwork alone, or they may want both you and the debtor to come to a hearing. In this case you will be told where and when the hearing is to be held.

Note that if the debtor is an individual and their address is on another court's patch, your claim will be transferred to that court, even if the judge decides not to hold a hearing. In that case you will be sent yet another form, N271: Notice of Transfer.

If there is a hearing and you choose not to attend, the judge may still make an order.

When the judge has decided – whether at a hearing or on the basis of the paperwork alone – you and the debtor will each be sent an order saying what the judge has decided. If it is different from the previous order, you will both be sent form N30(3): Judgment for Claimant After Re-determination.

As before, this orders the debtor to pay up, but does not actually guarantee you will get your money (see Chapter 8).

4 Admit part of the claim, disputing the balance

The debtor does this on form N9B: Defence and Counterclaim. They must then complete both this form and the Admission Form (N9A). You can now apply for a **default judgment** for the admitted amount only.

5 Dispute the whole of the claim

You cannot now apply for a default judgment, but if the debtor's grounds for dispute have, as the Civil Procedure Rules put it, 'no real prospect of succeeding', you may still be able to get a **summary judgment** (see flowchart, p 15).

6 Make a claim against you – a counterclaim

If this happens, you may still be able to get a **default judgment** if the debtor's claim is not a defence to the debt. You will, however, still have to defend the debtor's claim against you (outside the scope of this book; seek professional advice).

Plus – A slippery debtor can file an **acknowledgment of service** saying they intend to dispute all or part of the claim – this buys them breathing space, because they now have 28 days instead of 14 days from the date of service in which to file any defence.

Getting a default judgment

If you are entitled to a **default judgment**, then:

o   the day after the deadline, complete the Request for Judgment part of the Notice of Issue which the court has sent to you;

o   think carefully about how you want to be paid. Of course you want the money immediately, but it may be more realistic to accept an offer of instalments. Sign and date the form and return it to the court. There is no fee and you do not have to attend court.

The court will now send you your judgment and will also send copies to the defendant and the Register of County Court Judgments. Well done!

Be organised!

o   Always quote the case number on all your correspondence with the court.
o   Always keep copies of all written communications, both with the debtor and with the court.
o   Always keep file notes, with dates, of all meetings and telephone conversations.

Interest after judgment

The amount of your **judgment debt** will include any interest the court has awarded you up to that date. What about the interest from the date of judgment until the date when the debt is actually paid? Look again at pp 24–26 where we describe the three headings under which you can claim interest.

1 Contractual interest

You are entitled to interest from the date of judgment to the date of actual payment if *either*:

o   you were also entitled to claim **statutory** interest – that is, where your debtor was another business; *or*
o   the amount of the judgment debt is £5,000 or more.

2 Statutory interest

You are entitled to interest from the date of judgment to the date of actual payment.

3 Discretionary interest

You are entitled to interest from the date of judgment to the date of actual payment only if the judgment debt is £5,000 or more.

Rate of interest on judgment debts

In all three cases, the rate of interest on the judgment debt after judgment will be what is known as the 'judgment debt rate', which is currently 8% a year simple (that is, not compound).

Claiming interest on judgment debts

If you have to take **enforcement** proceedings (see Chapter 8) and you want to claim interest on the judgment debt (who wouldn't?), you have to include the interest claim in your application. You should include details of:

o   the sum on which you are claiming interest;

o   the dates from and to which you are claiming;

o   the rate of interest that applies (that is, 8% simple; see p 26).

7

Slugging it out in court

Many debtors will pay up on a small claim rather than face the hassle of **filing** a defence and appearing in court. But what if the debtor refuses to cave in?

In that case, the court will send you the debtor's response to your claim. This will take the form of either:

o   an **acknowledgment of service** (form N9). This just buys more time for the debtor to file a defence – which is now extended from 14 days to 28 days from the date the claim was issued. Make a note of the new deadline in your diary. If they fail to file a defence in time, apply for a **default judgment** (see p xvii) *immediately*;

or

o   a defence.

Look at this carefully. If you can see points where the debtor is mistaken, consider sending the court a 'Reply to the defence'. Remember what we said on p 24 about the burden of proof.

When the court sends you the debtor's defence, they will also send you and the debtor each an 'Allocation Questionnaire' (form N150). You can download a sample from the Court Service website. You must complete and return the Allocation Questionnaire to the court within the time limit stated on the form. The form mentions pre-action protocols, but have no fear! There is no specific pre-action protocol for debt proceedings (creditors' and debtors' lobbies have never been able to agree what to put in one!). The completed questionnaire will help the court to decide which **track** is appropriate to your claim.

Meanwhile, if it is obvious that the defence clearly has no merit at all, you can apply for a **summary judgment** straight away. An example where summary judgment is likely to be available is where the debtor's cheque has bounced and you are suing on the cheque. Use form N244, available from any court or on the Court Service website. You will need to prepare your paperwork and evidence because there will be a hearing of your application.

But what if a summary judgment is not an option, because the debtor's defence is not all hot air? You and the debtor will have to slug it out.

The court will send you what are called 'directions' telling you what you need to do before the trial. They will also set a date and time for the trial of your case.

Do your homework

Comply with the court's *directions*. These will always include a requirement for you to make a list of relevant documents and send it to the other side. The list of documents should include those which harm your case as well as those which help it. You may also have to write and exchange witness statements.

Preparation is the key to success. Think carefully about the following:

o   which documents you need, both to state your case and to refute the defence;

o   whether you need witnesses. If you do, check whether they are willing to attend the trial (many people will have urgent engagements elsewhere) and, even if the court does not require you to do so, prepare witness statements. The Court Service offers a leaflet: *I Have Been Asked to be a Witness – What Do I Do?* (available from any court, or from the Court Service website) which is worth reading.

You can include yourself as a witness, in which case write a witness statement for yourself. *Important*: always put a Statement of Truth (see p 27) at the end of each witness statement, which the witness should sign. Unwilling witnesses can be compelled to attend by a witness summons (form N20), but such witnesses tend to be hostile. A witness summons may, however, be appropriate where your witness is in employment and this is the best way for them to get the time off work. Note that where you summon a witness, you have to pay the witness's travel expenses and compensation for loss of time.

Compare your particulars of claim with the defence. Isolate any conflicts of fact and make sure that your witness statements get *your* version across.

o   Consider whether you need expert evidence from an independent professional. The need for this is not always obvious but if, for example, the defence asserts that the goods or service you supplied were defective, an expert can refute this.

o   Prepare what professionals call a 'trial bundle'. The last thing the trial judge will want is a complete rats' nest of papers dumped on their desk with no indication of what is there or why. A trial bundle is usually in the form of one or more A4 ring binders. Put the relevant papers into chronological order, number them consecutively and put a contents list, with page numbers, at the front. Provide four copies of the trial bundle – one for you, one for the judge, one for the defence and one for witnesses. Ask the debtor if there is anything they would like to include in your trial bundle. It is preferable to have just one bundle – not two competing ones.

o   In your own copy of the trial bundle, cross-reference the documents to the Particulars of Claim, the debtor's defence and the witness statements. This will enable you to explain the case to the judge and show the judge where to find the relevant documents as you go along. Judges really appreciate any help you can give them.

o   If the defence has raised points of law, look them up if you feel confident, or take legal advice if you don't. The court expects you to bring along a 'legal authority' – this is not a stout gentleman in a gown and wig, but either a copy of the relevant legislation or the case report you are relying on.

In court

Find out where the court is well before the trial date and consider going there beforehand, so that you know the route and how long it will take to get there. There is nothing worse than a desperate search around an unfamiliar city centre minutes before the trial is due to start. The Court Service website lists all the county courts; many have maps of the area and some even have virtual tours of the building.

Arrive slightly before the appointed time. Check in at the desk with the court usher, who will mark on the case list that you are present and will direct you to a waiting area.

1   Be prepared for a long wait. If you have to pre-pay for parking, put a generous amount in the machine.

2   Courts provide lavatories and drinks machines and very little else. Take something to read and a flask of decent coffee or a bottle of water.

3   Take a pen and a pad of A4 paper – if you don't have it, you're sure to need it. Take your trial bundles with you (although it is good practice to send copies to the debtor and the court in advance).

Last-minute deals

Nothing is certain in litigation. You might think your case is unanswerable, but are you living in the real world? Keep an open mind. Trials take unexpected twists and turns.

The time spent in the waiting area of the court can be put to good use in striking a last-minute deal. It is usually worthwhile accepting a discount on your claim in return for certainty.

If you are able to do a deal, it is wise at this late stage to put it into the form of what lawyers call a 'consent order' (which is where your A4 pad comes in). Write out the terms of the deal and check that the debtor agrees them. Then, when your case is called, you and the debtor should both go before the judge and say that you have settled the claim in principle and would like the terms put into a court order. Give the judge a copy of the agreement. If the judge approves it, they will make an order to that effect. The terms of the deal usually replace the original claim. The order is legally binding, so that if the debtor fails to pay up you can enforce the terms of the deal (not reactivate the original claim as such).

Appearing in court

We will assume that the court allocates your claim to the small claims **track**. Small claims courts are fairly informal. The case will normally be heard in the judge's chambers, which in practice means a book-lined room with a desk for the judge and a table where you, the debtor and any witnesses sit. As the claimant, you will normally sit on the right-hand side of the table as you look at the judge.

The judge will already have read the papers on the court file. This is where your trial bundle will come into its own.

The judge will be used to **litigants in person** and will not expect the same standards of eloquence from you as from a professional. They will probably ask you to set out your case in your own words. Address the judge as Sir or Madam and guide them through your trial bundle.

1   You may find it helpful to have a 'dry run' of the opening statement with a friend playing the part of the judge. The friend should be able to pick up on any inconsistencies.

2   This is a small claims court, not a courtroom drama. Resist any urge to emulate the hotshot lawyers in *Philadelphia*. Keep it understated.

3   Take a pocket calculator with you – to rework the debt and interest if that becomes necessary, or to refute the debtor's dodgy figures.

If the debtor gets difficult, perhaps interrupting, don't let it worry you and don't answer back. It could work to your advantage. If you stay calm and stick to the evidence, the judge will form a good impression of you and a bad one of the debtor. And *never* interrupt the judge!

Take notes as the case goes along. After the debtor has had their say, you will normally have another chance to comment on this. Be sure to highlight any inconsistencies, but be courteous about it.

The judgment will be given orally first, then confirmed in a written order. It is not necessarily the final word – remember that the debtor has a right of appeal!

For further details, see the Court Service guide: 'Coming to a court hearing? Some things you should know' (EX342 – W3), available from any court or from the Court Service website.

Finally, remember that this is only the briefest summary of court procedure. If all of this seems daunting, take professional advice. Even if it *doesn't* seem daunting, you may well need advice anyway.

8

Making it stick: enforcement

The *good news* is that you now have your judgment. The court has agreed that the debtor owes you money, and ordered the debtor to pay you.

The *bad news* is that having a judgment does *not* guarantee that you will actually get any money!

If, after you have obtained judgment, you are not paid promptly, various enforcement procedures are open to you.

These are:

1 **order to obtain information**

Not, strictly speaking, an enforcement procedure as such, but an interrogation session about the debtor's finances, which is useful if you need more information before deciding which weapon to use (see p 49).

2 **warrant of execution**

This gives the order for the court bailiffs to swing into action and is useful where the debtor has valuable belongings (see p 55).

3 **attachment of earnings**

This orders a sort of PAYE with you playing the part of the taxman – only useful where a debtor is in work (see p 61).

4 **third party debt order**

Use this where the debtor has money in the bank (see p 67).

5 charging order

This is a potent weapon where the debtor is a property owner, or has shares or other securities (see p 71).

6 appointment of equitable receiver

This can be suitable

o where the debtor is a landlord, because it enables you to divert the rents from the debtor to you via a third person (the equitable receiver); or

o where the debtor has a private pension (because you can't get an attachment of earnings order over a pension as opposed to a salary). However, the procedure is cumbersome, costly and outside the scope of this book. A **charging order** (see above) will usually be preferable where the debtor owns property.

Before you take any of these steps, however, do some serious thinking. Bear in mind that:

❷ enforcement will take time and effort on your part;

❷ there will be further court fees to pay (which get added on to the judgment debt but may, of course, never be recovered).

The Court Service offers useful leaflets on enforcement: access their website and click on 'Forms and Guidance'.

If Christmas comes early

Whichever enforcement procedure you choose, there is one rule: if you are lucky enough to receive any money direct from the debtor, *always tell the court*.

Is it worth it?

As we have said before, you cannot get blood out of a stone. A useful first step, therefore, is to find out whether the debtor *has the means to pay*. The debtor may already have provided information about their means if they have admitted your claim (there is space for this on the Admission Form which is provided by the court).

You can, in theory, obtain more information informally by writing direct to the debtor, but there is no guarantee that they will reply truthfully or at all. Otherwise, consider applying for an **order to obtain information**.

This used to be called an *oral examination*. It is a court order requiring the debtor to attend a question and answer session about their finances before an officer of the court. First, bear in mind that:

o   an order to obtain information is not in itself a method of enforcement;

o   it is not compulsory before enforcement action;

o   it does not get you any money there and then.

However, an order to obtain information may give you the facts you need to decide which method of enforcement to try. For example, you should be able to find out:

o   whether the debtor is in employment and what their earnings are – in which case an **attachment of earnings** order is an option;

o   whether the debtor has any valuable assets, in which case you might consider a **warrant of execution**;

o   whether the debtor owns any bricks and mortar, in which case a **charging order** is a possibility;

o   whether the debtor has savings, in which case you could opt for a **third party debt order**.

Since the debtor must verify to the court that the information that they give in the question and answer session is true, it is more likely to be reliable than would otherwise be the case.

Additionally, some people set great store by their financial privacy. The threat of having to reveal their secrets is enough to persuade them to pay up. Your debtor may be one of these.

The Court Service issues a helpful leaflet: *Order to Obtain Information – How Do I Apply for an Order?*, which you can get from your local court or download from the Court Service website. Click on 'Forms and Guidance' and home in on 'EX324'. The detailed rules about orders for information are enshrined in Part 71 of the Civil Procedure Rules, which you can study online on the Lord Chancellor's website.

Procedure

o   Get a copy of the application form. There are different forms depending on whether the debtor is an individual (N316 'Application for order that debtor attend court for questioning') or a company (N316A 'Application for order that officer of debtor company attend court for questioning'). Once again, you can obtain this from your local county court or download direct from the Court Service website – click on 'Forms and Guidance'.

o   Fill in the form – Rosy, the Phorm Phobic, filled one in and got it right first time.

1   If there is a particular line of investigation that you want the court to follow (for example, the debtor once bragged to you about his vintage car) there is provision for you to enclose a list of questions with the form. You can also ask the debtor to bring along specific documents. The questions which the court asks are in forms EX140 (for individuals) and EX141 (for companies). We suggest that you obtain copies for yourself (details as above) and read these questions before starting to compile your own.

2   You can ask for the questioning to take place before a judge, but your request is not likely to be granted unless you can show that the debtor is particularly devious. However, if you do manage to get a judge involved you *must* attend the hearing and ask all the questions yourself, and the proceedings will be taped.

  –   Prepare to pay the court fee of £40 using cash, postal order or a cheque made out to HMPG.

- Send or take the form and the fee to the court where you obtained judgment – unless the case has been transferred to a different court in the meantime, in which case send or take the form and fee there. The court will then make an order for the debtor to attend at their 'home' court (see p 16).

If you are an individual **litigant in person**, the court will serve the order to attend on the debtor and send a copy to you. If you are a company, they will send you the order to attend and you will have to arrange **personal service** of the order on the debtor not less than 14 days before the hearing date. Personal service does not mean serving the document yourself. You can arrange this with a **process server** (look in the Yellow Pages under 'Detective Agencies'). The court is not involved at this stage.

The court will not send the debtor the list of questions, nor any supplementaries you have added. There is a case for copying the questions to the debtor before the hearing, because otherwise they may protest that the relevant papers are at home! If, however, you plan a surprise attack on a particular asset, it may be wiser not to give advance warning.

There is yet more paperwork to be done before anyone can interrogate your debtor. The court will want to know the following:

o that, if you were responsible for **personal service** of the order, this has been done (either by you or by a process server (see above);

o that the debt is still unpaid;

o that, if the debtor has asked for travel expenses, you have paid them. Note that if they ask for travel expenses, you must pay a 'reasonably sufficient' amount to cover the cost of getting to the court by public transport.

You must give this information in an **affidavit** on form EX550 (available from your local court or the Court Service website. This form must be *sworn* (see p xv) and sent to the court where the hearing is to take place not less than two days before the hearing if you are not attending; otherwise take it along to the hearing. If you instructed a process server to effect personal service, they must provide a separate *affidavit of service.*

The hearing

The questioning will usually be conducted in private by an officer of the court. The hearing is likely to be relatively informal. All the same, the debtor will be under oath.

Unless the hearing is before a judge (see above), the court officer will ask the debtor the questions on form EX140 (for individuals) or form EX140A (for companies), as well as any questions you have added to the list.

You are under no obligation to attend, except when the hearing is before a judge. However, being there in person will give you an opportunity to press in with unlisted 'supplementaries' such as 'If money is so tight, how did you manage to pay for your skiing holiday?' and to see how the debtor reacts to each question: body language can be very revealing.

The court officer will make a written record of the debtor's replies and ask them to sign it, although if the hearing is before a judge there will be a tape recording but no written record.

What happens if the debtor does not show?

Failure to attend without good excuse may amount to contempt of court, for which the sentence could be a short spell in prison. In practice, the court gives the debtor the benefit of the doubt first time around. The court sets another time and date for the hearing – and the debtor usually gets a suspended committal order ('Go to court or go to jail!'). If you are responsible for **service**, you must arrange **personal service** as before.

Questioning a limited company

You can find out about a limited company's financial situation by asking for one of its directors to attend using form N316A (see above). This may require a little gentle sleuthing.

The company's headed paper will often give the names of directors, but not their addresses. Have no fear! – you can find out directors' names *and addresses*, as well as their occupations, date of appointment and dates of birth, from Companies House (see 'Useful contacts' for the general enquiries number). There is a fee of £4 – per company, not per director – to have the details posted to you, or £5 to have them faxed (payable over the telephone by credit card).

Unfortunately, some devious and/or secretive companies name other companies as their directors. In this case, all you will get is the name and address of those companies, which won't help much especially if they are registered offshore.

The procedure is the same as for an individual debtor, but the hearing may take place at the director's 'home' court if this is not the same as for the company's place of business.

Note: Where your debtor is a firm or partnership rather than a limited company, apply to question one of the partners using form N316.

Warrant of execution

Not an appointment with the headsman, but rather an authority from the court to send the **bailiffs** to the debtor's home or business premises, to either collect money to pay the **judgment debt** or to take away the debtor's belongings to sell at auction. This is called *levying distress*. In *The Mill on the Floss*, by George Eliot (1860), several burly bailiffs force their way into the debtor's home and carry off everything of value. Bailiffs have changed their methods since then. Today's bailiffs are likely to write or telephone first, to give the debtor an opportunity to pay the debt. They are not allowed actually to break into the debtor's home, although they can force entry into business premises as long as these do not include residential accommodation (so a debtor living over their shop might be safe).

Bailiffs' (and sheriffs' officers') powers

Bailiffs can call at the debtor's home at any reasonable time to seize goods.

They are not allowed to break into the premises by force, but they can legally enter the property 'peacefully' (the law's word, not ours) through open windows or unlocked doors. Once inside, they are allowed to go into every room and can force their way into other parts of the property. For example, they can force their way into separate buildings such as sheds and garages regardless of whether the debtor let them into the house itself.

Bailiffs can seize goods that are not actually in the debtor's home, such as items at the debtor's workplace or in a friend's house, or cars or motorbikes parked outside.

Once inside, the bailiffs *cannot* take away:

o **basic household and personal belongings** which the debtor and their family need for day-to-day living (TVs, videos and hi-fis are not yet regarded as necessities and are therefore fair game);

o **belongings which the debtor needs in order to work** – which can include tools, computers and vehicles (but not a vehicle used simply to drive to and from work, so the bailiffs might leave a van but take a car);

o **items which do not belong to the debtor**, or of which the debtor is not the sole owner, or which are on lease or HP;

o **items which are not worth the cost of removing and selling**.

Note that the bailiffs will deduct from the proceeds of sale the costs of removing, storing and selling the goods. There may be precious little left for you. *A warrant of execution is a waste of time and money if the debtor has no money and no valuable belongings.*

There is an element of 'shock and awe' and also public humiliation about a visit from the bailiffs. The mere threat of this might persuade a sensitive debtor to pay up rather than suffer the *Mill on the Floss* treatment – and be the talk of the neighbourhood. Also, the court will add the bailiffs' fees to the money the debtor owes.

Applying for a warrant of execution in the county court

Note: the procedure set out below applies to judgment debts of less than £5,000.

For amounts over £5,000, you will need the High Court equivalent (outside the scope of this book) unless the debt relates to an agreement regulated under the Consumer Credit Act 1974, which can only be enforced in the county court. You can choose to use the High Court if the debt is more than £600.

Complete the court request form N323, available from your local county court or on the Court Service website. Read the explanatory leaflet, EX322, also available from the court or on the Court Service website. Note that there is space on the form for you to give any information you have about the debtor's belongings and their value. The bailiffs are not detectives and can only work from the information you give them. If you want results, do your homework.

Interest

If you want to claim interest on the **judgment debt**, you have to include the interest claim in your application. You should include details of:

o   the sum on which you are claiming interest;

o   the dates from and to which you are claiming;

o   the rate of interest that applies (that is, 8% simple; see p 26).

Bone up on bailiffs too. Download leaflet EX322: *About Bailiffs and Sheriffs' Officers* from the Court Service website before you start proceedings.

Note that if you are planning to issue a warrant of execution in the High Court, you will need a further document called a 'certificate of judgment'. You ask the court for this using form 293A: 'A combined certificate of judgment to enforce the judgment by a writ of *fi fa*'. You can get this form from any court, or download it from the Court Service website.

However, the Court Service leaflet warns 'High Court procedure is different from county courts and can be complicated and more expensive', and advises you to get advice before you start. We agree with them. If a lot of money is at stake, you cannot afford to let your debtor escape on a technicality.

Fi fa is short for *fieri facias*, a convoluted piece of Latin which translates roughly as 'thou shalt make it to be done'.

- Prepare to pay the court fee, using cash, postal order or a cheque made out to HMPG. The county court fee is currently £30 where you are seeking to recover not more than £125, and £50 for amounts over £125.
- If the judgment debt is payable by instalments, you can ask the bailiffs to collect *either* the whole amount of the judgment debt *or* the unpaid instalments, and the fee will be in accordance with the amount you ask the bailiffs to collect.
- Send or take the form and the fee to the court where you obtained the judgment.

A note on Money Claim Online

If you submitted your claim online and got your judgment that way, you can also apply for your warrant of execution online and pay the fee by credit card.

What happens next?

Within 10 working days of receiving your form, the court sends an ultimatum to the debtor – pay the full amount to the court in seven days, or else. The 'or else' is that if the debtor does not pay, the bailiffs will call and try to collect the money. Failing that, they will try to seize goods for sale at auction.

The court should report to you on the outcome, and if you do not hear from them within, say, one month of sending off your form, you should ring and ask for an update.

If the bailiffs are unsuccessful, the court will tell you why. This is usually because the bailiffs cannot find the debtor or any of the debtor's belongings, or any belongings worth selling.

Can you ask the bailiffs to try again?

Yes. There is a special form, N445, available as before. You can use this to update the information you have given the bailiffs, such as any change of the debtor's address or any new information about their belongings which comes to light. You must also pay an extra fee of £20.

A warrant lasts one year, although you can apply to extend the warrant's life before the year is up. This will cost you the same fee as for the original warrant.

Can the debtor grab some breathing space?

Yes. The debtor can apply to the court to suspend the warrant. Typically, they make a last-ditch offer to pay, either in full or by instalments. If this happens, the court will let you know. You must then decide whether to:

o agree the suspension and accept the offer;

o agree the suspension and ask for more – in which case the warrant will be suspended and an officer of the court will decide how much the debtor can pay and order accordingly;

o refuse to agree the suspension – in which case you will have to attend a court hearing to explain your reasons. The hearing will be in private, before a district judge – call the judge 'Sir' or 'Madam'.

A note on 'walking possession agreements'

This is an agreement between the debtor and the bailiff, and is another way for the debtor to have a chance to breathe. On the bailiff's first visit, the debtor signs a list of possessions which the bailiffs will allow the debtor to keep as long as the debt is paid within an agreed time. If the debtor fails to pay, the bailiffs can come back – entering by force if necessary – and seize the goods.

Whose goods?

A not infrequent problem with warrants of execution is that disputes arise about who really owns the goods that the bailiffs seize. Sometimes these disputes result in court proceedings – in which case, take professional advice.

The bailiffs are allowed to seize *jointly owned* goods, in which case the proceeds are divided between you and the other owner, typically the debtor's partner.

You can learn more about warrants of execution from the Court Service leaflet: *About Bailiffs and Sheriffs' Officers*, EX322, available from your local court or from the Court

Service website as before. The detailed rules are enshrined in the County Court Rules 1981 order 26, available on the Lord Chancellor's website.

Attachment of earnings

This is a court order for a **judgment debt** to be paid by instalments out of the debtor's earnings from employment. 'Earnings' here includes private pensions, but not state old-age or disability pensions. Think of attachment of earnings as private PAYE, with you as the taxman. It takes an employer to dock the debtor's wages at source, so attachment of earnings is *not* relevant if the debtor is:

o   out of work;

o   self-employed;

o   a firm (sole trader or partnership); or

o   a limited company.

Furthermore, you cannot get an attachment of earnings order against a debtor who is a merchant seaman or who is in the army, navy or air force. There are special rules for these people and you will need to take legal advice.

Even if the debtor is in employment, you cannot apply for an attachment of earnings order unless:

o   you have a judgment debt for at least £50; *and*

o   if the judgment debt is payable immediately, the debtor has failed to pay it; *or*

o   if the judgment debt is payable by instalments, the debtor has fallen behind with the payments.

Is it worth your while?

Just as people on the very lowest incomes pay no tax, the court will not make an attachment of earnings order against a debtor who cannot afford to pay.

The court will get the debtor to fill in a 'Statement of Means' similar to the one on p 123 and will allow the debtor to retain enough income to keep themselves and their family. This is called the 'protected earnings rate'. The court will not make an attachment of earnings order if the debtor's income is less than the protected earnings rate.

If the debtor's income is more than the protected earnings rate, the court will make an attachment of earnings order but the amount of the instalments will depend upon the debtor's ability to pay.

Procedure

o   If applicable, apply to transfer the case to the debtor's 'home' court – see the standard letter on p 116 and on the website.

o   Complete the court request form N337, available from your local county court or on the Court Service website.

If you want to claim interest on the **judgment debt** (who wouldn't?), you have to include the interest claim in your application. You should include details of:

  o   the sum on which you are claiming interest;

  o   the dates from and to which you are claiming;

  o   the rate of interest that applies (that is, 8% simple; see p 26).

o   Prepare to pay the court fee of £50 using cash, postal order or a cheque made out to HMPG.

You do not have to pay a fee if someone else already has an attachment of earnings order against the same debtor and you ask for your debt to be collected under the existing order (called *consolidation* (see 'A note on consolidated orders', below)), so do some checking before you part with your £50. Ask the debtor's home court to search their Attachment of Earnings Index to find out whether an attachment of earnings order is already in force. There is no fee for this and you might be able to do it over the telephone. Otherwise there is a form, N336, available as above.

o   Send or take form N337 and the fee to the debtor's 'home' court. This is the local county court for the area where the debtor lives. If you do not know which court to use, your own local county court will tell you.

What happens next?

The court tells the debtor either to pay up or to fill in a Statement of Means form (which the court will supply, and which is similar to ours on p 123). If the debtor does not reply, the court can ultimately order the arrest of the debtor and make them fill in the form at the court.

From the information supplied in the Statement of Means, the court calculates the 'protected earnings rate' and, if the debtor's earnings exceed this, the amount of the instalments that will be docked from their wages.

Copies of the order are then sent to:

o   the debtor's employer, so that they know how much to deduct and when;

o   the Centralised Attachment of Earnings Payments System (CAPS), which will collect the payments and pass them on to you;

o   the debtor;

o   you.

Can the debtor grab some breathing space?

Yes. The debtor can apply to the court to suspend the order. Many debtors will apply to do so if they do not want their employer to find out that they are in debt. Typically, the debtor makes a last-ditch offer to the court to pay the debt direct to you, either in full or by instalments. If this happens, the court will decide whether to suspend the order and you will be informed of their decision.

If the attachment of earnings order is suspended but the debtor does not keep up the payments, you can ask the court to reinstate the order. You need yet another form for this, N446, available as before. There is no fee.

Can you have your say?

Yes. If you think any decision made by the court is wrong (for example, because of false information from the debtor), you can ask them to reconsider. This might happen if, for example:

o   no attachment of earnings order is made;

o   the amount of the instalments seems too low; or

o   the order is suspended.

For this, you will need yet another form, N244, available as before, and you *must* get this back to the court with a fee of £50 within 16 days of the date of the relevant order. Make sure you tell the court why you are objecting.

Your request may lead to a court hearing, held in private before a district judge – call the judge 'Sir' or 'Madam'.

What happens if the debtor becomes unemployed?

The attachment of earnings order lapses, but it can be reinstated if the debtor gets another job. You need form N446, available as above. There is no fee.

What happens if the debtor changes jobs?

You have to find out the name and address of the new employer (not always easy, but consider an **order to obtain information** (see p 49). You can then ask the court to notify the new employer. The form to use is N446 (see above). There is no fee.

A note on consolidated orders

This is the order you can get for free if another creditor has been there before you (see above). A consolidated order can be made where two or more people have applied for attachment of earnings orders against the same debtor. The effect is to simplify the employer's role. Instead of coping with a multiplicity of orders, the employer takes a single amount from the debtor's wages and sends it to CAPS (see above). The court then sends you your share. Note, however:

- ○ the *advantage* of a consolidated order is that there is no up-front court fee, although the court deducts 10% of all monies received from the employer.

- ○ the *disadvantage* is that you may well receive less money, less often.

Third party debt order

A **third party debt order** is a court order for the debtor's money in a bank or building society account to be paid direct to you to pay a **judgment debt**. You can also get a third party debt order over money that is owed by someone else to the debtor. So, if you know for a fact that Mr X owes your debtor money, you can get the court to order Mr X to pay *you* the amount of the judgment debt before handing anything over to the debtor.

You cannot apply for a third party debt order unless:

o you have a judgment debt; *and*

o if the judgment debt is payable immediately, the debtor has failed to pay it; *or*

o if the judgment debt is payable by instalments, the debtor has fallen behind with the payments.

Note that

o your order will be ineffective unless there is actually money in the debtor's bank at the time the bank receives the order;

o your order will not catch money which comes into the account *after* the order is made;

o you cannot get a third party debt order over a *joint* bank account;

o you cannot get a third party debt order over salary/wages accruing but not actually due for payment. (If the debtor is in work, an **attachment of earnings** order will usually work better.)

There are two significant problems with third party debt orders, namely:

o finding out in sufficient detail where the debtor keeps their money. You may, for example, have the debtor's bank details on cheques which you have received from them previously, but if the cheques bounced in the past, is there really any money there now? (Otherwise, try an **order to obtain information** (see p 49));

o getting at the money before the debtor gets wind of your plans and spirits it away.

So, if a third party debt order is going to work, you need reliable intelligence, immaculate timing and the element of surprise. In theory, a third party debt order is supposed to work like the perfect ambush. In practice, it is more like the Keystone Cops – more often than not, the debtor and the money will be one step ahead of you.

Procedure

Complete the court request form N349, which you will find on the Court Service website – click on 'Forms and Guidance'; don't forget to access the accompanying leaflet too. Note that there is a Statement of Truth on the form, so take care that the information you provide is accurate.

Remember that if you want to claim interest on the **judgment debt**, you have to include the interest claim in your application. You should include details of:

o the sum on which you are claiming interest;

o the dates from and to which you are claiming;

o the rate of interest that applies (that is, 8% simple; see p 26).

The court will not make an order on a 'speculative application' – in box 5 of the form you have to give evidence to support your belief that there is, or will be, money in the debtor's account. If you are short of information, consider an **order to obtain information**.

o Prepare to pay the court fee of £50, using cash, postal order or a cheque made out to HMPG.

o Send or take the form and the fee to the court dealing with your case.

- As timing is crucial, tell the court the date (ideally the day after the debtor's pay day – you see how important good intelligence is!) on which you want them to make the order.

What happens next?

The third party debt procedure comes in three stages.

Stage 1: Interim third party debt order

This will order the bank to freeze the money in the debtor's account and also order them to carry out a search to identify all accounts in the debtor's sole name. The bank must give the details to you and to the court within seven days. This is done *ex parte* – without the debtor's prior knowledge (obviously!).

The court sends you a copy of the interim order. This gives the date for the hearing (see below). Check with the court whether they will send copies of the interim order to the bank and to the debtor, or whether they expect you to **serve** the papers yourself. If the court expects you to do so, you should serve the interim order, plus a copy of your application and any documents in support, on:

- the bank, so that they receive the papers not less than 21 days before the hearing; and
- the debtor, so that they receive the papers not less than seven days before the hearing.

Personal service is not necessary: first-class post is sufficient, but keep a note of the date, time and place of posting or delivery and record this in a 'certificate of service' (on form N215 – download one from the Court Service website, as before). Leave at least seven days between serving the bank and service on the debtor. Take your certificate of service to the hearing with you.

Stage 2: Court hearing

There will be a hearing before the district judge, which you *must* attend. The purpose of the hearing is to decide whether the interim order should be made final. If the debtor or the bank objects, they must send the court, and you, written evidence before the hearing date. Common grounds for objection are that there is no money in the account or, if there is, that it belongs to someone else!

The hearing will be in private, before a district judge – call the judge 'Sir' or 'Madam' (see Chapter 7 for information about attending court).

If there is no money in the account or the account is overdrawn, the bank must notify you and the court. You will then know you are onto a loser. You should withdraw your application before the hearing. Otherwise, you may have to pay the costs of the debtor and/or the bank. Note that in any case the bank can make an administration charge – currently £55 – for dealing with the order, and this has priority over your judgment debt.

Stage 3: Final third party debt order

Assuming you are successful at the hearing, the court will order the bank to take money from the debtor's account and pay it to you.

Pleading poverty

The debtor can make a one-off application to the court for what is known as a 'hardship payment order'. This will enable the debtor to keep some of the money in the account if they can show that they and their family would otherwise be unable to meet ordinary day to day living expenses. You will usually receive advance warning of this application, and there will be a hearing. However, in cases of exceptional urgency the court can make a hardship payment order without telling you first.

Charging order

This is a court order by which a **judgment debt** is **secured** against the debtor's home or other bricks and mortar. Think of a **charging order** as a type of mortgage with you in the position of the lender, although you are not paid by instalments and you will have to wait until the property is sold to get your money. You can also get a charging order over investment assets such as shares.

In contrast to a **third party debt order** (where you are shooting at a moving target), a charging order is aimed at assets such as bricks and mortar, which may be harder for the debtor to conceal or dispose of quickly. The exception is, of course, shares, which can be sold instantly (but see below on *stop notices*).

Do you really want a charging order?

Consider:

o The property may already be heavily mortgaged. An **order to obtain information** (see p 49) will tell you more about this.

o The court may not be willing to grant a charging order for a small judgment debt.

o The debtor may not be the sole owner of the property. You can still get a charging order, *but only over the debtor's share of the property*. It is more difficult to get an order to sell the property without the co-owner's agreement – take professional advice.

Do you really want to do it yourself?

Consider:

o In practice, the procedures are complicated and it might make sense to get a lawyer to act for you. For example, you will usually need details of the property from HM Land Registry and the application is inevitably more complicated where the debtor is a co-owner of the property.

o The charging order is only the first stage – it only prevents the debtor from selling the property; it doesn't pay you off. You still need a separate order for sale (outside the scope of this book) before you get your money.

Procedure for a charging order over real estate

o Apply to HM Land Registry for details of the debtor's property. You need firstly the title number for the property – apply on Land Registry form SIM, obtainable from your local Land Registry (see 'Useful contacts').

Once you have the title number, you can apply for a copy of the register for the property, including the filed plan (that is, the Land Registry's official plan of the property). Use Land Registry form OC1 (see below). Copies of the register are known as *office copy entries*. The Land Registry fees are £4 for each office copy entry and £4 for each copy of the plan. You have to apply to the land registry which deals with the property – to find out the appropriate one, telephone HM Land Registry and press 1 for general enquiries, or go to their website.

Not all properties are yet registered. If it transpires that the property concerned is unregistered, you will need to get an **order to obtain information** to get the details you need. Take professional advice.

o Apply for the charging order using form N379 if the debtor is the sole owner of the property. Otherwise you should use form N244, available from the

Court Service website. If the debtor co-owns the property with their spouse or partner (this will show up in your Land Registry entries), you must name them on the application form. You can download both forms from the Court Service website as before – click on 'Forms and Guidance' for the forms themselves and the accompanying leaflet). Take care that the information you provide is accurate and remember that you must sign a Statement of Truth to that effect.

Remember that if you want to claim interest on the **judgment debt**, you have to include the interest claim in your application. You should include details of:

– the sum on which you are claiming interest;

– the dates from and to which you are claiming;

– the rate of interest that applies (that is, 8% simple; see p 26).

o Prepare to pay the court fee of £50, using cash, postal order or a cheque made out to HMPG.

o Send or take the form and the fee to the court that is dealing with your case.

What happens next?

The charging order procedure is in four stages (three compulsory stages and one optional, but very wise, one).

Stage 1

o The court puts a temporary charge (an 'interim charging order') on the property, which will remain in force until there is a hearing. The interim charging order is made before the debtor knows anything about it.

o The court sends you a copy of the interim charging order, which is on form N86 (not available on the Court Service website – it will be sent to you). This gives the date for the hearing (see below).

o Check with the court whether they will send the debtor a copy of the charging order, or whether they expect you to **serve** the order yourself. If the court expects you to do so, you should serve the interim order, plus a copy of your application and any documents in support, so that they receive the papers not less than 21 days before the hearing, on:

- the debtor;

- any co-owner of the property; and

- anyone else the court directs – who will usually be a lender who already has a mortgage over the property.

Personal service is not necessary: first-class post is sufficient, but keep a note of the date, time and place of posting or delivery and record this in a certificate of service (on form N215 – download one from the Court Service website as before). Take the certificate of service along to the hearing.

Stage 2: Register the order

As soon as you have your interim charging order, you should tell the land Registry. The procedures for registering charging orders, and all the forms, changed in November 2003, when the Land Registration Act came into force. There are four forms: AN1, UN1, RX1 and K1. There is a wealth of information on the Land Registry website (www.landreg.gov.uk). Call the helpline (0870 90 88 061), which has been set up to deal with queries arising from the changes.

Stage 3: The hearing

There will be a hearing before the district judge, which you *must* attend. The purpose of the hearing is to decide whether the interim order should be made final. If the debtor objects, they must send written evidence to the court and to you before the hearing date.

The hearing will be in private, before a district judge – call the judge 'Sir' or 'Madam'.

Stage 4: The final order

If your application is successful, the court converts the interim order into a final charging order. To protect your position before the property is sold, you should register the final charging order with the Land Registry if you have not already done so (see Stage 2 above). Remember that this gives you the equivalent of a mortgage over the property, and you will need to make a further application for the property to be sold (outside the scope of this book).

Procedure for a charging order over shares/securities

The procedure is similar, but the form is different! You need form N380, which you can get from any court or download from the Court Service website.

As soon as you receive the interim order, send a copy to the company in which the debtor owns the shares. This has the effect of freezing the shares to prevent the debtor from selling them, and also stops the company from paying the debtor any dividends or interest pending the hearing. At the hearing, check that the final order will include what is known as a 'stop notice', which will prevent the company registering any transfer of the shares or paying any dividends or interest without warning you. The stop notice will, of course, only be effective if you serve a copy of the final order on the company.

Bankruptcy for beginners

In medieval Italy, a moneylender who could not pay his debts had his bench or counter - his *banco* - *rup*tured or broken by his creditors. He was put out of business.

Today, a **bankruptcy** order is a formal declaration by the court that an individual is insolvent. The effect is that the bankrupt person's financial affairs are put into the hands of a **licensed insolvency practitioner**, who collects in the **bankrupt**'s assets and shares them out among the **creditors**.

After a period of time, the debtor is allowed to keep all *new* earnings and all *new* assets. In effect, the debtor's slate is wiped clean except for assets which the debtor concealed from their creditors, and also certain debts (such as maintenance payments and state benefits obtained by fraud) to which bankruptcy does not apply.

At the time of writing, the rules about bankruptcy are changing in the light of the Enterprise Act 2002, which received royal assent on 7 November 2002 and which makes far-reaching changes to corporate and personal insolvency law. While the Act has received royal assent, this does not mean that all the changes it makes will have been brought into force by the time you read this book.

Prior to the Act, bankrupts stayed that way for either two or three years, depending on the amount of money they owed. There was no distinction between really dishonest bankrupts and financially incompetent or downright unlucky ones. Also, there was no limit on the time allowed to the **Trustee in Bankruptcy** (**TiB**) to deal with the bankrupt's home, so the TiB could bide their time until the bankrupt's home had increased in value to make it worth selling it off to repay the debts.

Under the new Act:

o   the bankruptcy period will be reduced so that an individual can be discharged from bankruptcy after only 12 months rather than two or three years;

o   the TiB must deal with the family home within three years of the date of the bankruptcy order, compared with no time limit at the time of writing. If the TiB 'times out', the family home reverts to the bankrupt.

o   a new Bankruptcy Restriction Order (BRO) regime will be brought into force to keep dodgy bankrupts out of business for between two and 15 years, depending on how badly they have behaved.

These provisions of the Enterprise Act 2002 are expected to kick in early in 2004.

In the meantime, during the bankruptcy there are restrictions on the bankrupt's financial activities. However, today's bankrupt, unlike the Italian moneylender, can still continue to earn their living – with certain restrictions (a bankrupt cannot be a company director, practise as a GP or a solicitor or be an MP, for example) as long as they use their own name and do not borrow (the official term is *pledge credit for*) more than £250 without telling the lender about their bankruptcy. Also, today's bankrupt keeps their bench – that is, the tools of their trade – and also basic household and personal belongings which the bankrupt and their family need for day to day living.

What, you may ask, happens if an undischarged bankrupt is earning megabucks? Can they keep it all? Well, the court can, where appropriate, make an **income payments order** against a bankrupt whose earnings during the bankruptcy period justify this.

A recent case involved a famous sportsman who went spectacularly bankrupt. He generated a lot of media attention and made a lot of money appearing on chat shows and working as a commentator. The court made an income payments order against him and the proceeds went to his creditors.

Note that the court will not make an income payments order which would reduce the bankrupt's income below what is seen to be the reasonable domestic needs of the bankrupt and their family.

Normally an income payments order ceases when the debtor is discharged from their bankruptcy, although under the Enterprise Act 2002 an income payments order will be able to run for up to three years even if the bankruptcy order itself ends in the meantime.

Note that you can use bankruptcy procedure in two ways:

o   as an alternative to a court claim for debt, or

o   as a method of enforcing a judgment debt.

Do you really want to bankrupt your debtor?

'*Can* pay, *won't* pay' debtors (see p 7), particularly those in business or a profession, are the likeliest target. Bankruptcy would cramp their style and they would prefer to avoid it. The *threat* of bankruptcy, in the form of a **statutory demand** (see Chapter 14), involves no court fees and may well make the debtor pay up in order to stay in business.

However, this threat doesn't work with everyone. A real no-hoper may welcome bankruptcy. He has been in deep trouble financially for a long time. Now you come along and save him the cost of bankrupting himself! This is currently a £140 court fee – waived if he is on benefits – plus a £300 compulsory Official Receiver's deposit, all payable in cash to the court (well, would *you* accept a cheque from a potential bankrupt?). In as little as one year's time (barring gross misconduct – see the BRO, p 78) he will be discharged and he will be free to start again with a clean slate.

Whilst the *threat* of bankruptcy may concentrate your debtor's mind wonderfully and get you a quick result, bear in mind that:

- bankruptcy proceedings are limited to debts of £750 or more. If you are owed less than £750 you can gang up with other small creditors to get over the £750 hurdle;

- bankruptcy proceedings are not suitable where the debtor has genuine grounds for disputing your claim (although, of course, the debtor cannot dispute a judgment debt unless he applies to the court to have it cancelled, or appeals);

- taking bankruptcy proceedings does not get you to the front of the queue of creditors.

Creditors with valid security (shares, bricks and mortar and so on) are the lucky ones. They can realise the secured assets to get their money. All creditors – including **secured creditors** to the extent that their security is worth less than the amount they are owed – can claim in the bankruptcy, but their position in the queue is rigidly defined.

After the **licensed insolvency practitioner** has received their fees and any **preferential debts** have been paid in full, everyone else is paid proportionately from what's left, according to the value of their claims. *So if you bankrupt somebody you may be going to a lot of effort and expense for someone else's benefit (and even (see above) for the bankrupt's benefit).*

We mentioned expense earlier. Compared with suing for debt in the county court, bankruptcy proceedings are expensive. The court fee for a **creditor**'s (as opposed to a debtor's) bankruptcy application is £180. You also have to make an advance payment to the Insolvency Service of £300, although in theory this may be refundable later if the bankrupt's assets allow. So you will have to pay out £480 with no guarantee of any return on your money.

Additionally, your £300 is refunded if no bankruptcy order is made and the petition is withdrawn. The obvious scenario would be if the debtor paid you in full.

Sabre rattling: the statutory demand

A **statutory demand** says 'Pay up – or else!'

It is a formal demand for payment of a debt, as the first stage of bankruptcy proceedings. A statutory demand must be made on the official form, and **personal service** on the debtor is obligatory.

Personal service does not mean serving the document yourself. You can arrange this with a **process server** (look in the Yellow Pages under 'Detective Agencies'). The court is not involved at this stage.

You do not *have* to serve a statutory demand if you already have a **judgment debt** *and* you have issued a **warrant of execution** *and* the **bailiffs** have entered the debtor's premises but come away empty-handed. You can still, however, *choose* to do so, and as this exception is of limited scope it is in fact sensible always to do so.

Given that the *threat* of bankruptcy is often more effective than the bankruptcy order itself (see above), serving a statutory demand on a debtor is always a useful way to build up the pressure. Unless you pay a process server to do it for you, serving a statutory demand costs you nothing – there is no court fee at this stage. Some creditors might use the time and place of service to embarrass the debtor. You can probably think of several times and places which would have the desired effect!

Suing for bankruptcy (individuals)

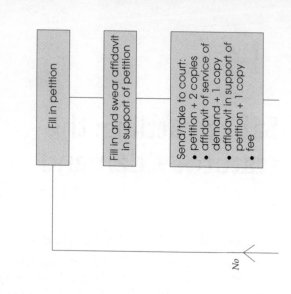

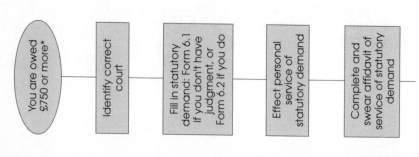

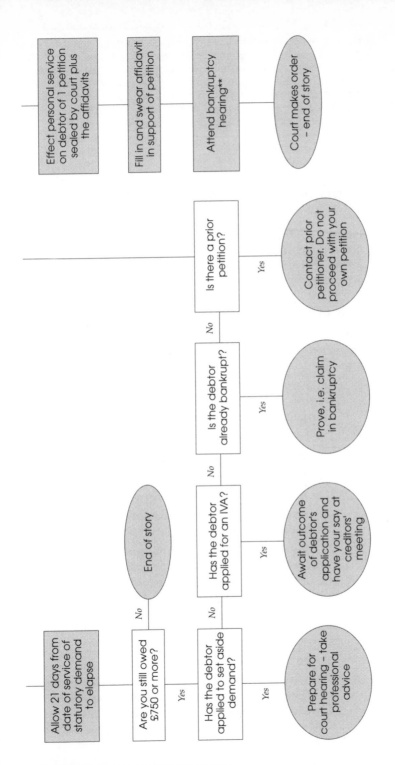

* Alternatively, you and other creditors acting together are owed £750 or more
** You may also want a representative present if the petition is defended – take legal advice if this occurs

Beware! Before you serve a statutory demand, be sure that the debtor cannot challenge the validity or amount of the debt. If the debtor makes a successful court application to **set aside** your demand, you will usually end up paying the debtor's legal costs in the case as well as your own. These may be substantial if there is a lengthy court hearing. If the debtor makes an application to set aside your demand, take legal advice *immediately*.

Procedure – the 'statutory demand' stage

Fill in the official form. You must use form 6.1 if you do not already have a judgment debt against the debtor, or form 6.2 if you do have one. Examples of the forms are given here, and you can download blank forms from the Insolvency Service website – just click on the form you want in the forms menu.

Note: You must use the correct form – nothing else has the legal clout you need. Fill the form in carefully, and bear in mind the following points.

1   You cannot claim for any debt to the extent that it is secured, for example, if you have the benefit of a mortgage over the debtor's property).

2   The Particulars of Debt must state:

   o   when the debt was incurred;

   o   how it arose; *and*

   o   the exact amount due at the date of demand.

   It is sensible to include a calculation and to attach copies of relevant contracts or invoices.

3   You have to include the name and address of the court which will deal with the case. This is usually the debtor's local county court, but check with the court whether they deal with bankruptcies – not all county courts do. If they don't, they will tell you where to go. County courts are listed in the telephone directory under 'Courts'.

   A note on London

   If, for the greater part of the previous six months, the debtor has lived or carried on business in the 'London Insolvency District', you must start proceedings in the **High Court**. The London

Insolvency District, broadly speaking, comprises the City of London, the City of Westminster and the London boroughs.

If you think this may apply to your debtor, you can check whether you should be using the High Court by telephoning the Bankruptcy Section on 0207 947 6448. If the High Court does have jurisdiction, the address to put on your statutory demand is:

Bankruptcy Court
Royal Courts of Justice
Thomas More Building
The Strand
London WC2A 2LL

Although High Court proceedings are generally outside the scope of this book, have no fear! For straightforward bankruptcy matters the procedures and fees are the same as for county courts, and you can use the forms provided in this book and on our website. The main difference is that bankruptcy petitions in the High Court have to be filed *in person*, not posted (see 'High Court procedure' below).

4   You have to sign the statutory demand form – and the signature must be that of an individual (not a trade name, etc).

5   You have to date the form – in practice, put this in shortly before service.

Now effect **personal service**. To do this, you (or your **process server** – see below) must leave the statutory demand with the debtor. In practice, this means *handing it to the debtor* or, if they will not accept it, *laying it at their feet*. You should tell the debtor what the document is, particularly if it is in an envelope. If you do not want to effect personal service yourself, arrange for a competent process server with professional indemnity insurance (look in the Yellow Pages under 'Detective Agencies') to do it for you.

If your debtor is keeping out of the way and you cannot find them, there are alternative procedures for service which are outside the scope of this book. Take professional advice.

---

o   Take a note of the precise date, time and venue of service, and incorporate these details into an **'affidavit** of service' (see form 6.11 on the Insolvency Service website). If you instruct a process server, make sure they provide a completed affidavit of service for you. The affidavit must be signed in front of a solicitor or a court official.

What happens next?

The debtor has 21 days from the date of **personal service** to respond to your statutory demand. The debtor has four options:

1   Pay up in full. End of story.
2   Apply to the court within 18 days for the statutory demand to be **set aside** – the obvious response if the debt is disputed. This will lead to a court hearing. Take professional advice.
3   Apply for an **individual voluntary arrangement** – often abbreviated to IVA – a private deal for the repayment of debts between an individual debtor and their creditors, supervised by a **licensed insolvency practitioner**. People with IVAs are allowed to carry on trading. An IVA application has the effect of putting bankruptcy proceedings on hold. Further details are outside the scope of this book.
4   Lie low and say nothing – in which case you need to consider whether you want to go on to bankruptcy proceedings.

Form 6.1

Rule 6.1

Statutory Demand under section 268(1)(a) of the Insolvency Act 1986. Debt for Liquidated Sum Payable Immediately

Notes for Creditor

- If the Creditor is entitled to the debt by way of assignment, details of the original creditor and any intermediary assignees should be given in part C on page 3.

- If the amount of debt includes interest not previously notified to the debtor as included in the debtor's liability, details should be given, including the grounds upon which interest is charged. The amount of interest must be shown separately.

- Any other charge accruing due from time to time may be claimed. The amount or rate of the charge must be identified and the grounds on which it is claimed must be stated.

- In either case the amount claimed must be limited to that which has accrued due at the date of the demand.

- If the creditor holds any security the amount of debt should be the sum the creditor is prepared to regard as unsecured for the purposes of this demand. Brief details of the total debt should be included and the nature of the security and the value put upon it by the creditor, as at the date of the demand, must be specified.

- If signatory of the demand is a solicitor or other agent of the creditor the name of his/her firm should be given

Warning

- This is an **important** document. You should refer to the notes entitled "How to comply with a statutory demand or have it set aside".

- If you wish to have this demand set aside you must make application to do so **within 18 days** from its service on you.

- If you do not apply to set aside **within 18 days** or otherwise deal with this demand as set out in the notes **within 21 days** after its service on you, you could be made bankrupt and your property and goods taken away from you.

- Please read the demand and notes carefully. If you are in any doubt about your position you should seek advice **immediately** from a solicitor or your nearest Citizens Advice Bureau.

DEMAND

To

Address

This demand is served on you by the creditor:

Name

Address

The creditor claims that you will owe the sum of £
full particulars of which are set out on page 2, and that it is payable immediately and, to the extent of the sum demanded, is unsecured.

The creditor demands that you do pay the above debt or secure or compound for it to the creditor's satisfaction.

[The creditor making this demand is a Minister of the Crown or a Government Department, and it is intended to present a bankruptcy petition in the High Court in London.]
[Delete if inappropriate]

Signature of individual
Name
(BLOCK LETTERS)

Date

*Delete if signed by the creditor himself.

*Position with or relationship to creditor

*I am authorised to make this demand on the creditor's behalf.
Address

Tel No   Ref.

N.B. The person making this demand must complete the whole of pages 1, 2 and parts A, B and C (as applicable) on page 3.

Particulars of Debt
(These particulars must include (a) when the debt was incurred, (b) the consideration for the debt (or if is there is no consideration the way in which it arose) and (c) the amount due as at the date of this demand).

Notes for Creditor
Please make sure that you have read the notes on page 1 before completing this page.

Note:
If space is insufficient continue on page 4 and clearly indicate on this page that you are doing so.

DEBT RECOVERY

Part A

Appropriate Court for Setting Aside Demand

Rule 6.4(2) of the Insolvency Rules 1986 states that the appropriate court is the court to which you would have to present your own bankruptcy petition in accordance with Rule 6.40(1) and 6.40(2). In accordance with those rules on present information the appropriate court is [the High Court of Justice]

[County Court]

(address)

Any application by you to set aside this demand should be made to that court.

Part B

The individual or individuals to whom any communication regarding this demand may be addressed is/are:

Name _____

(BLOCK LETTERS)

Address _____

Telephone Number _____

Reference _____

Part C

For completion if the creditor is entitled to the debt by way of assignment

	Name	Date(s) of Assignment
Original creditor		
Assignees		

How to comply with a statutory demand or have it set aside (ACT WITHIN 18 DAYS)

If you wish to avoid a bankruptcy petition being presented against you, you must pay the debt shown on page 1, particulars of which are set out on page 2 of this notice, within the period of **21 days after** its service upon you. Alternatively, you can attempt to come to a settlement with the creditor. To do this you should:

- inform the individual (or one of the individuals) named in part B above immediately that you are willing and able to offer security for the debt to the creditor's satisfaction; or
- inform the individual (or one of the individuals) named in part B immediately that you are willing and able to compound for the debt to the creditor's satisfaction.

If you dispute the demand in whole or in part you should:

- contact the individual (or one of the individuals) named in part B immediately.

THERE ARE MORE IMPORTANT NOTES ON THE NEXT PAGE

If you consider that you have grounds to have this demand set aside or if you do not quickly receive a satisfactory written reply from the individual named in part B whom you have contacted you should **apply within 18 days** from the date of service of this demand on you to the appropriate court shown in part A above to have the demand set aside.

Any application to **set aside the demand (Form 6.4 in Schedule 4 to the Insolvency Rules 1986) should be made within 18 days from the date of service upon you and be supported by an affidavit (Form 6.5 in Schedule 4 to those Rules) stating the grounds on which the demand should be set aside. The forms may be obtained from the appropriate court when you attend to make the application.**

REMEMBER!—   From the date of service on you of this document
                   (a) you have only 18 days to apply to the court to have the demand set aside, and
                   (b) you have only 21 days before the creditor may present a bankruptcy petition

DEBT RECOVERY

Form 6.2

Rule 6.7

Statutory Demand under section 268(1)(a) of the Insolvency Act 1986. Debt for Liquidated Sum Payable Immediately Following a Judgment or Order of the Court

Notes for Creditor

- If the Creditor is entitled to the debt by way of assignment, details of the original creditor and any intermediary assignees should be given in part C on page 3.

- If the amount of debt includes interest not previously notified to the debtor as included in the debtor's liability, details should be given, including the grounds upon which interest is charged. The amount of interest must be shown separately.

- Any other charge accruing due from time to time may be claimed. The amount or rate of the charge must be identified and the grounds on which it is claimed must be stated.

- In either case the amount claimed must be limited to that which has accrued due at the date of the demand.

- If the creditor holds any security the amount of debt should be the sum the creditor is prepared to regard as unsecured for the purposes of this demand. Brief details of the total debt should be included and the nature of the security and the value put upon it by the creditor, as at the date of the demand, must be specified.

- Details of the judgment or order should be inserted, including details of the Division of the Court or District Registry and court reference, where judgment is obtained in the High Court.

- If signatory of the demand is a solicitor or other agent of the creditor the name of his/her firm should be given.

*Delete if signed by the creditor himself.

Warning

- This is an **important** document. You should refer to the notes entitled "How to comply with a statutory demand or have it set aside".

- If you wish to have this demand set aside you must make application to do so **within 18 days** from its service on you.

- If you do not apply to set aside **within 18 days** or otherwise deal with this demand as set out in the notes **within 21 days** after its service on you, you could be made bankrupt and your property and goods taken away from you.

- Please read the demand and notes carefully. If you are in any doubt about your position you should seek advice **immediately** from a solicitor or your nearest Citizens Advice Bureau.

DEMAND

To

Address

This demand is served on you by the creditor:

Name

Address

The creditor claims that you owe the sum of £
full particulars of which are set out on page 2, and that it is payable immediately and, to the extent of the sum demanded, is unsecured.
By a Judgment/Order of the   court in proceedings entitled Case
Number   between
Plaintiff and
Defendant it was adjudged/ordered that you pay to the creditor the sum of £
and £   for costs.

The creditor demands that you do pay the above debt or secure or compound for it to the creditor's satisfaction.

[The creditor making this demand is a Minister of the Crown or a Government Department, and it is intended to present a bankruptcy petition in the High Court in London.]
[Delete if inappropriate]

Signature of individual
Name
(BLOCK LETTERS)

Date

*Position with or relationship to creditor

*I am authorised to make this demand on the creditor's behalf.
Address

Tel No   Ref.

N.B. The person making this demand must complete the whole of pages 1, 2 and parts A, B and C (as applicable) on page 3.

6.2 Statutory Demand under section 268(1)(a) of the Insolvency Act 1986. Debt for Liquidated Sum Payable Immediately Following a Judgment or Order of the Court 11/99

Particulars of Debt
(These particulars must include (a) when the debt was incurred, (b) the consideration for
the debt (or if is there is no consideration the way in which it arose) and (c) the amount
due as at the date of this demand).

Notes for Creditor
Please make sure that you have
read the notes on page 1 before
completing this page.

Note:
If space is insufficient continue
on page 4 and clearly indicate
on this page that you are doing
so.

6.2 Statutory Demand under section 268(1)(a) of the Insolvency Act 1986. Debt for Liquidated Sum Payable Immediately Following a Judgment or Order of
the Court 11/99

DEBT RECOVERY

Part A
Appropriate Court for Setting Aside Demand

Rule 6.4(2) of the Insolvency Rules 1986 states that the appropriate court is the court to which you would have to present your own bankruptcy petition in accordance with Rule 6.40(1) and 6.40(2).

Any application by you to set aside this demand should be made to that court, or , if this demand is issued by a Minister of the Crown or a Government Department, you must apply to the High Court to set aside if it is intended to present a bankruptcy petition against you in the High Court (see page 1).

In accordance with those rules on present information the appropriate court is [the High Court of Justice].
[County Court]
(address)

Part B
The individual or individuals to whom any communication regarding this demand may be addressed is/are:

Name _____
(BLOCK LETTERS)
Address _____

_____
Telephone Number _____
Reference _____

Part C
For completion if the creditor is entitled to the debt by way of assignment

	Name	Date(s) of Assignment
Original creditor		
Assignees		

THERE ARE IMPORTANT NOTES ON THE NEXT PAGE

6.2 Statutory Demand under section 268(1)(a) of the Insolvency Act 1986. Debt for Liquidated Sum Payable Immediately Following a Judgment or Order of the Court 11/99

How to comply with a statutory demand or have it set aside (ACT WITHIN 18 DAYS)

If you wish to avoid a bankruptcy petition being presented against you, you must pay the debt shown on page 1, particulars of which are set out on page 2 of this notice, within the period of **21 days after** its service upon you. However, if the demand follows (includes) a judgment or order of a County Court, any payment must be made to that County Court (quoting the Case No.). Alternatively, you can attempt to come to a settlement with the creditor. To do this you should:

- inform the individual (or one of the individuals) named in part B above immediately that you are willing and able to offer security for the debt to the creditor's satisfaction; or

- inform the individual (or one of the individuals) named in part B immediately that you are willing and able to compound for the debt to the creditor's satisfaction.

If you dispute the demand in whole or in part you should:

- contact the individual (or one of the individuals) named in part B immediately.

If you consider that you have grounds to have this demand set aside or if you do not quickly receive a satisfactory written reply from the individual named in part B whom you have contacted you should **apply within 18 days** from the date of service of this demand on you to the appropriate court shown in part A above to have the demand set aside.

Any application to set aside the demand (Form 6.4 in Schedule 4 to the Insolvency Rules 1986) should be made within 18 days from the date of service upon you and be supported by an affidavit (Form 6.5 in Schedule 4 to those Rules) stating the grounds on which the demand should be set aside. The forms may be obtained from the appropriate court when you attend to make the application.

REMEMBER!— From the date of service on you of this document
(a) you have only 18 days to apply to the court to have the demand set aside, and
(b) you have only 21 days before the creditor may present a bankruptcy petition

---

6.2 Statutory Demand under section 268(1)(a) of the Insolvency Act 1986. Debt for Liquidated Sum Payable Immediately Following a Judgment or Order of the Court 11/99

Serious swordsmanship: the bankruptcy petition

You rattled your sabre (see Chapter 14) but the debtor failed to respond to your statutory demand within the time limit. You can now go ahead and bankrupt them. Here's how to do it. Note that it involves some heavy duty form-filling and you must get every stage absolutely right, or the judge will throw your petition out.

o   Check with the debtor's 'home' county court (see p 16) whether they deal with bankruptcies (not all do). If they don't, they will tell you where to go.

o   Check that your debtor is not already bankrupt or about to become bankrupt. You can do this by searching the Individual Insolvency Register (see 'Useful contacts').

o   Allow 21 days to pass after serving the **statutory demand**, then check with the court whether the debtor has applied either to **set aside** your demand or to obtain an **individual voluntary arrangement** (IVA).

At the same time, check with the court whether there is already a bankruptcy petition in existence – if there is, *do not* continue with your own petition. Instead, contact the existing petitioner. You may be able to join forces.

o   Fill in the Bankruptcy Petition, form 6.7, which you will find on the Insolvency Service website. See pp 128–31 for a guide to completing it. Fill it in carefully, and note the following:

    –   the petition itself does not require dating, signing or witnessing;

- you can only claim the debt as stated in your statutory demand (no 'Oh, and by the way …');
- if you have a county court judgment, you need to confirm that the debtor has not paid any money to the court.

o Fill in the Affidavit of Truth of Statements in Bankruptcy Petition (form 6.13 on the Insolvency Service website, as before) which provides the evidence to back up your petition. If more than four months have passed since you served your statutory demand, you must explain the reason for the delay. As the form is an affidavit, remember that you must sign it in front of a solicitor (who will charge a small fee) or a court official (who will do it for free). If you have not already done so, you must do the same with your Affidavit of Service of Statutory Demand.

o Prepare to pay the court fee of £180 and the Official Receiver's fee of £300. You make one payment of £480, using cash, postal order or a cheque made out to HMPG.

o Send or take (*note that the High Court insists on the latter*) the following documents to the court that is dealing with the case:
- Bankruptcy Petition (form 6.7) plus two copies;
- Affidavit of Service of Statutory Demand (form 6.11) plus one copy;
- Affidavit in Support of the Bankruptcy Petition (form 6.13) plus one copy;
- the fee.

Make sure you keep a copy of everything for your own file.

o If your paperwork is in order, the court will issue your petition – that is, put an official stamp on it and give it back to you for **personal service** on the debtor.

Effect **personal service** of the petition on the debtor (see above), and at the same time give the debtor a copy of the Affidavit in Support of the Petition (form 6.13). Fill in your Affidavit of Service of the Bankruptcy Petition (form 6.17, available on the Insolvency Service website as before). This must be signed in front of a solicitor or a court official.

High Court procedure

There are two points to note if you are taking bankruptcy proceedings in the High Court (see 'A note on London', p 84).

o The High Court still expects you to **file** your petition and accompanying documents *in person*, and not to post them (although this no longer appears to be an express requirement of the rules).

o The High Court requires you to check that there have been no bankruptcy petitions against the debtor within the previous 18 months and, if there have, that any such petitions have been dismissed (the Insolvency Service can tell you only about actual bankruptcies, not near misses). You need to obtain this information from the High Court's own database, for which you will be charged £5. Here's how.

1 Go to the information desk at the Royal Courts of Justice, the Thomas More Building (see 'Useful contacts'), collect a free map and ask for the Fees Room. There you pay £5 and receive a search ticket.

2 Take your ticket to Room 211, second floor. You will be allotted 15 minutes at a computer terminal.

3 Armed with your search result, you can then file your petition in the same room. Ask the staff to check your paperwork for you.

Some county courts may also require this information – practice varies from court to court. Most will do a free search for you either over the telephone or by post. Ask!

What happens next?

The court sets a hearing date for the petition. You *must* attend – take copies of all the paperwork with you.

Additionally, the court will want to know whether the debt is 'still due and owing'. You can reassure them by bringing with you a Certificate that Debt Still Due and Owing, which should take the following form:

> I certify that to the best of my knowledge and belief the debt on which the petition is founded is still due and owing and has not been paid or secured or compounded.
>
> Signed ....…......
>
> Dated ....…......

You should also take with you to the hearing a list of creditors as follows:

List of creditors intending to appear on the hearing of the bankruptcy petition

> IN THE HIGH COURT OF JUSTICE
> *OR* .... COUNTY COURT
> NO .... OF 20 ......
>
> In Bankruptcy
>
> Re .... *(name of debtor as in title of petition)*
>
> In the matter of a bankruptcy petition filed on .... 20 ......
>
> The following Creditors have given notice that they intend to appear on the hearing of the above-mentioned petition on .... 20 ......
>
>
>
> Name of Creditor ....
>
> Address of Creditor ....
>
> Creditor's Solicitors ....
>
> Whether intending to support or oppose the petition ....

Obviously if you are the only creditor intending to appear, you will say so on the form.

The hearing will be in private, before a district judge – call the judge 'Sir' or 'Madam'. The court will inform you beforehand if the debtor decides to defend the petition, in which case you should take professional advice.

Note that if your petition is unsuccessful and the court does not make a bankruptcy order, you may be liable to pay the debtor's legal costs.

If you are successful, however, and a bankruptcy order is made, you cannot ask the bankrupt to pay you direct. You have to apply to the Official Receiver, or whoever else is appointed to manage the bankrupt's financial affairs.

Liquidation

Liquidation is to *companies* what **bankruptcy** is to *individuals*. The essential considerations are the same. In particular:

o the threat of liquidation, in the form of a **statutory demand**, is usually more effective than the proceedings themselves, and much cheaper;

o liquidation proceedings are not suitable where the debtor has genuine grounds for disputing your claim;

o liquidation does not get you to the front of the queue of creditors.

Liquidation is different from bankruptcy in the following respects.

o Liquidation means what it says – a liquidated company ceases to exist, whereas bankruptcy is not intended to be fatal!

o The £750 minimum level of debt does not apply if you already have a **judgment debt** against the company debtor *and* you have failed to get satisfaction through enforcement procedures (but ask yourself if it would ever be cost effective to take liquidation proceedings for a debt of less than £750!). Do not, in any case, seek to liquidate a company owing you less than £750 without taking legal advice: the applicable law is even more arcane than usual.

o There is no facility for the company debtor to apply to the court to **set aside** any statutory demand. Instead, the company can apply to the court to restrain presentation of the petition.

o You do not *have* to serve a statutory demand, and you may *choose not to do* so if time is of the essence (the company debtor has 21 days to pay after the demand is served).

If you do choose to serve a statutory demand, it must be left at the company's registered office (see below). **Personal service** on a director or other senior officer of the company is incorrect.

○　County courts have jurisdiction only where the company debtor's paid-up share capital does not exceed £120,000.

○　The county courts in the London Insolvency District (see p 84) do not have jurisdiction to hear company liquidations, and the application has to be started in the **High Court**. Although High Court proceedings are generally outside the scope of this book, have no fear! For straightforward matters, the procedures and fees are the same as for county courts and you can use the forms on the Insolvency Service website. The address of the High Court is on p 143.

It takes a lot of form-filling to wind up a company. Luckily all the forms are on hand as part of an Insolvency Service leaflet: *Dealing With Debt: How to Wind Up a Company That Owes You Money*, available from any Official Receiver's office or from the Insolvency Service website, as before.

The 'statutory demand' stage

○　Fill in the official form (form 4.1) – an example of what it looks like is given here for your reference. Follow the guidelines for the statutory demand stage in bankruptcy on pp 84–86 above. It is vital to get the name of the company *exactly right* – it must be the same as the name registered at Companies House.

Form 4.1

Rule 4.5

Statutory Demand under section 123(1)(a) or 222(1)(a) of the Insolvency Act 1986

Warning
- This is an **important** document. This demand must be dealt with **within 21 days** after its service upon the company or a winding-up order could be made in respect of the company.
- Please read the demand and notes carefully.

Notes for Creditor

- If the Creditor is entitled to the debt by way of assignment, details of the original creditor and any intermediary assignees should be given in part B on page 3.

- If the amount of debt includes interest not previously notified to the company as included in its liability, details should be given, including the grounds upon which interest is charged. The amount of interest must be shown separately.

- Any other charge accruing due from time to time may be claimed. The amount **or rate** of the charge must be identified and the grounds on which it is claimed must be stated.

- In either case the amount claimed must be limited to that which will have accrued due at the date of the demand.

- If signatory of the demand is a solicitor or other agent of the creditor the name of his/her firm should be given

*Delete if signed by the creditor himself.

DEMAND

To

Address

This demand is served on you by the creditor:

Name

Address

The creditor claims that the company will owe the sum of £ full particulars of which are set out on page 2.

The creditor demands that the company do pay the above debt or secure or compound for it to the creditor's satisfaction.

Signature of individual

Name
(BLOCK LETTERS)

Date

*Position with or relationship to creditor

*I am authorised to make this demand on the creditor's behalf.

Address

Tel No   Ref.

N.B. The person making this demand must complete the whole of this page, page 2 and parts A and B (as applicable) on page 3.

Particulars of Debt
(These particulars must include (a) when the debt was incurred, (b) the consideration for the debt (or if is there is no consideration the way in which it arose) and (c) the amount due as at the date of this demand).

Notes for Creditor
Please make sure that you have read the notes on page 1 before completing this page.

Note:
If space is insufficient continue on reverse of page 3 and clearly indicate on this page that you are doing so.

DEBT RECOVERY

Part A

The individual or individuals to whom any communication regarding this demand may be addressed is/are:

Name _____

(BLOCK LETTERS)

Address _____

Telephone Number _____

Reference _____

Part B

For completion if the creditor is entitled to the debt by way of assignment

	Name	Date(s) of Assignment
Original creditor		
Assignees		

How to comply with a statutory demand

If the company wishes to avoid a winding-up petition being presented it must pay the debt shown on page 1, particulars of which are set out on page 2 of this notice, within the period of **21 days after** its service upon the company. Alternatively, the company can attempt to come to a settlement with the creditor. To do this the company should:

- inform the individual (or one of the individuals) named in part A above immediately that it is willing and able to offer security for the debt to the creditor's satisfaction; or
- inform the individual (or one of the individuals) named in part A immediately that it is willing and able to compound for the debt to the creditor's satisfaction.

If the company disputes the demand in whole or in part it should:

- contact the individual (or one of the individuals) named in part A immediately.

REMEMBER! The company has only 21 days after the date of service on it of this document before the creditor may present a winding-up petition.

o   Effect **service** of the statutory demand by leaving it at the company debtor's registered office.

You may later have to prove that this was done, so do not send your demand by post. To be safe, take the statutory demand round personally and put it through the letterbox, keeping a note of the time and date you do so. Or pay a **process server** to do it for you – and make sure they give you an Affidavit of Service after they have done the deed.

The registered office is often different from the company's trading address, but it must be in England or Wales. To find out a company's registered office address, call Companies House.

If the registered office address is obviously not a trading address for the company, deliver or post a copy of the demand to their trading address as well.

The 'liquidation' stage

The *Chancery Guide* (Chancery is the division of the court which deals with company insolvency) says: 'A winding up petition should not be presented when it is known that a debt is disputed in good faith ... The court may order the petitioner to pay the company's costs of a petition based on a disputed debt on the indemnity basis.'

This problem should not arise if you have a **judgment debt** against the company, because a judgment debt cannot be disputed unless the company applies to **set aside**, or appeals.

o   Allow 21 days to pass.

o   Check whether someone else has already filed a petition. You do this by searching the Central Index (details in 'Useful contacts'). If the answer is 'yes', contact the petitioner; you might be able to join forces.

o   If there is no prior petition, fill in your Petition using form 4.2. The information about the company required under headings 1 to 4 inclusive is all available from Companies House. Copies of the form are available from the Insolvency Service website.

o Fill in the **affidavit** verifying the winding-up petition (form 4.3), which provides the evidence to back up your petition.

o Prepare to pay the fees. For liquidation of a limited company, the court fee is £180 and the Insolvency Service fee is £500. You make one payment of £680, using cash, postal order or a cheque made out to HMPG.

o Send or take the following documents to the court which is dealing with the case:

    – Statutory Demand (form 4.1) plus one copy;

    – Winding-up Petition (form 4.2) plus three copies (one for the company, one for the court and two for you);

    – Affidavit Verifying Winding-up Petition (form 4.3) plus one copy;

    – the fee.

If your paperwork is in order, the court will **issue** your Petition – that is, put an official stamp on it and give three copies back to you (one for you to keep, one for you to **serve**, and one for you to enclose with your Affidavit of Service – see below).

Effect **personal service** of the original petition (that is, the one impressed with the court seal) on the company debtor. In the case of a company, personal service means leaving the petition with a director or other officer or employee of the company. You should, if possible, do this at the company's registered office – but see below.

Immediately after serving the petition, you must send the court an Affidavit of Service. There are two forms:

o use form 4.4 if you served at the company's registered office;

o use form 4.5 if you served at the company's principal place of business.

You can access the forms on the Insolvency Service website – make sure you use the correct form. A sealed copy (that is, with the court seal on it) of the petition must be included as an exhibit with your affidavit.

You must also advertise the petition in the *London Gazette* on one occasion only. Get out your diary and start working out time scales. The advertisement must appear

o   not less than seven 'business days' after the petition has been served on the company, *and*

o   not less than seven 'business days' before the hearing date.

A 'business day' is any Monday to Friday, excluding Christmas Day, Good Friday and Bank Holidays – for practical purposes, any day on which the county court office is open. The *London Gazette* comes out every weekday. (You can visit the *London Gazette* website (see 'Useful contacts') if you can read their murderously small print.)

You cannot choose your own wording for the advertisement. There is yet another form for this: form 4.6. It appears as a tear-off page at the end of the Insolvency Service's leaflet *Dealing with Debt: How to Wind Up a Company That Owes You Money*, available from any Official Receiver's office or from the Insolvency Service website, as before.

Send the advertisement, together with your cheque for £36.80 inclusive of VAT (details in 'Useful contacts'), or order and pay for the ad online at the *London Gazette* website giving your credit card details. Tell them the date you wish the advertisement to appear and remember to give them at least two days' notice.

Finally, you need to file a 'certificate of compliance', yet another form: 4.7. This appears as a tear-off page at the end of the Insolvency Service's leaflet *Dealing with Debt: How to Wind Up a Company That Owes You Money*.

File form 4.7 with the court *at least five days* before the hearing date, together with a cutting from the *London Gazette* showing your advertisement. This shows the court that you have jumped through the appropriate hoops.

What happens next?

You need to file two further forms:

o form 4.9, Notice of Intention to Appear on Petition; and

o form 4.10, List of Persons Intending to Appear on the Hearing of the Petition.

Both forms appear in a tear-off version at the end of the Insolvency Service's leaflet *Dealing With Debt: How to Wind Up a Company That Owes You Money*.

Obviously if you are the only creditor intending to appear, you will show that on the forms.

If the company decides to dispute your petition, they will file and serve evidence at least seven days before the hearing – in which case take legal advice. Otherwise, you should be successful and an order will be made to put the company into compulsory liquidation. Whether all this time, effort and expense will get you your money is, of course, another matter!

You can find more information about liquidation in the Insolvency Service leaflet as mentioned above.

Sample letters

The documents that follow are examples only, and they also appear on the website:

www.cavendishpublishing.com/pocketlawyer

You can download Word documents from the website and tailor them to your needs.

Contents

From Pickwick Papers Limited
Paper Place
Eatanswill
Kent EA12 1MF

To Mr R Nupkins
24 Promise Lane
Scoffantipple
SC29 1RB

[date]

Dear Mr Nupkins

Stationery Supplies

I refer to my company's invoice of [date] for £_____
in respect of stationery supplied to your firm. Under
our standard terms of business, payment should
have been made within 28 days of the date of
invoice. We are entitled to interest for late payment.

Would you please settle this bill within the next
seven days. You should of course ignore this letter if
you have paid before it reaches you.

Yours sincerely

Samuel Pickwick

Samuel Pickwick
Director
Pickwick Papers Limited

Yellow warning

From Pickwick Papers Limited
To Mr R Nupkins

[*date*]

Dear Mr Nupkins

Stationery Supplies

I refer to my company's unpaid invoice of [*date*] for
£ _____ in respect of stationery supplied to your
firm. I am concerned that you have not responded
to my reminder of [*date*].

Could you please settle this bill within seven days. If
you have difficulty in paying, please contact me
immediately.

Yours sincerely

Samuel Pickwick

Samuel Pickwick
Director
Pickwick Papers Limited

Red warning: Letter of Claim

From Pickwick Papers Limited
to Mr R Nupkins

[*date*]

Dear Mr Nupkins

<u>Stationery Supplies – Unpaid Bill</u>

I refer to my company's invoice of [*date*] for £____ in respect of stationery supplied to your firm; and to my reminders of [*date*] and [*date*], to which you have not replied.

I must ask you to settle this bill within the next seven days. If you fail to do so, I shall take legal action against you without further warning to recover the debt together with interest and costs. You should note that county court judgments are registered and may make it difficult for you to obtain credit in the future.

I enclose for ease of reference copies of the original contract and the relevant invoice.

If you have difficulty in paying, please contact me immediately.

Yours sincerely

Samuel Pickwick

Samuel Pickwick
Director
Pickwick Papers Limited

Summing up debtor's proposals for payment

From Pickwick Papers Limited
to Mr R Nupkins

[*date*]

Dear Mr Nupkins

Stationery Supplies – Unpaid Bill

I refer to our telephone conversation of [*date*]. You told me that you had been off work with an injured hand (unfortunately, the one you sign cheques with; and your firm has no other authorised signatory). I am glad that you are now recovered and back at your desk.

You offered to pay the debt by instalments of £____ per month starting on [*date*] and to provide post-dated cheques for the purpose. I am agreeable to this arrangement, provided you keep up the payments. If you fail to do so, the whole amount owed will immediately become due and payable. The unpaid balance will bear interest at a rate of ____ % per annum.

I look forward to receiving the first payment and the post-dated cheques.

Yours sincerely

Samuel Pickwick

Samuel Pickwick
Director
Pickwick Papers Limited

Asking the court to transfer the case to the debtor's home court

Sadly, Mr Nupkins failed to keep his promises and Mr Pickwick had to sue him in the county court. He started the case off in his home court (Eatanswill County Court) but later needed to transfer the case to Mr Nupkins' home court (Scoffantipple County Court).

From Pickwick Papers Limited
To the Court Manager, Eatanswill County Court
[*address*]
Claim No

[*date*]

Dear Sir

Pickwick v Nupkins, Claim No

I should be grateful if you would kindly transfer this claim to the Scoffantipple County Court, which is Mr Nupkins's local county court. Thank you for your assistance in this matter.

Yours faithfully

Samuel Pickwick

Samuel Pickwick
Director
Pickwick Papers Limited

Sample forms

Sample Particulars of Claim (page 2 of form N1)

These particulars of claim assume that the debt is contractual. You should give brief details of the contract terms:

o   the date of contract;

o   the type of contract (whether written or oral);

o   the nature of goods or services provided;

o   the price;

o   other relevant terms, such as time allowed for payment.

You should also provide the date of invoice, the amount of any payments made and the balance outstanding. If you are claiming interest, you must say so – see p 24.

Where the contract is written, you should attach a copy of the contract. In any event, attach a copy of your invoice.

In the example below, Pickwick Papers Limited is claiming from Mr Nupkins the sum of £500 representing the amount he owes for stationery which Pickwick Papers Limited have supplied to him (note that Mr Nupkins has already paid £100 of the original £600 bill).

Claim Form

In the SCOFFANTIPPLE COUNTY COURT

	for court use only
Claim No.	
Issue date	

Claimant

PICKWICK PAPERS LIMITED
PAPER PLACE
EATANSWILL
KENT EA12 1MF

TEL: 01202 123 123

SEAL

Defendant(s)

MR R NUPKINS
1 PROMISE LANE
SCOFFANTIPPLE
SC29 1RB

TEL: 01909 456 456

Brief details of claim

PAYMENT OF MONEY OWED FOR SUPPLY OF GOODS

Value

£500

Defendant's name and address	MR R NUPKINS 1 PROMISE LANE SCOFFANTIPPLE SC29 1RB		£
		Amount claimed	525.15
		Court fee	50.00
		Solicitor's costs	0.00
		Total amount	575.15

The court office at

is open between 10 am and 4 pm Monday to Friday. When corresponding with the court, please address forms or letters to the Court Manager and quote the claim number.
N1 Claim form (CPR Part 7) (01.02)   *Printed on behalf of The Court Service*

Claim No.	

Does, or will, your claim include any issues under the Human Rights Act 1998? ☐ Yes ☑ No

Particulars of Claim ~~(attached)~~ ~~(to follow)~~

THE CLAIMANT - PICKWICK PAPERS - IS A STATIONERY RETAILER. BY A WRITTEN AGREEMENT DATED 1 JUNE 2004 (COPY ATTACHED), THE CLAIMANT AGREED TO SUPPLY THE DEFENDANT - MR R NUPKINS - WITH 30 REAMS OF PERFUMED PAPER FOR £600 INCLUSIVE OF VAT. THE CLAIMANT DULY SUPPLIED THE PAPER AND INVOICED THE DEFENDANT ON 1 JULY 2004 UNDER INVOICE NO. PP2000 (COPY ATTACHED).

ON 1 AUGUST 2004 HE DEFENDANT PAID £100, BUT DESPITE REPEATED REQUESTS FOR PAYMENT, THE DEFENDANT HAS NOT PAID THE BALANCE OF THE INVOICE.

THE CLAIMANT HAS A CONTRACTUAL RIGHT TO INTEREST UNDER CLAUSE 3.5 OF THE AGREEMENT AT A RATE OF 12%. INTEREST IS CLAIMED FROM: 29 JULY 2004 TO TODAY, 28 DECEMBER 2004 BEING 153 DAYS. TOTAL INTEREST TODAY IS: £25.15. THE CONTINUING DAILY RATE OF INTEREST FROM TODAY IS 16p.

THE CLAIMANT ASKS FOR:

1. THE SUM OF £500
2. INTEREST OF £25.15
3. CONTINUING INTEREST AT A DAILY RATE OF 16p UNTIL JUDGMENT OR EARLIER PAYMENT.

Statement of Truth
*(I believe)(The Claimant believes) that the facts stated in these particulars of claim are true.
* I am duly authorised by the claimant to sign this statement

Full name   SAMUEL PICKWICK (OF PICKWICK PAPERS LIMITED)

Name of claimant's solicitor's firm ----

signed   *Samuel Pickwick*   position or office held DIRECTOR

*(Claimant)~~(Litigation friend)~~~~(Claimant's solicitor)~~   (if signing on behalf of firm or company)

*delete as appropriate

Claimant's or claimant's solicitor's address to which documents or payments should be sent if different from overleaf including (if appropriate) details of DX, fax or e-mail.

Notes for claimant on completing a claim form
Further information may be obtained from the court in a series of free leaflets.

- Please read all of these guidance notes before you begin completing the claim form. The notes follow the order in which information is required on the form.
- Court staff can help you fill in the claim form and give information about procedure once it has been issued. But they cannot give legal advice. If you need legal advice, for example, about the likely success of your claim or the evidence you need to prove it, you should contact a solicitor or a Citizens Advice Bureau.
- If you are filling in the claim form by hand, please use black ink and write in block capitals.
- Copy the completed claim form and the defendant's notes for guidance so that you have one copy for yourself, one copy for the court and one copy for each defendant. Send or take the forms to the court office with the appropriate fee. The court will tell you how much this is.

Notes on completing the claim form

Heading

You must fill in the heading of the form to indicate whether you want the claim to be issued in a county court or in the High Court (The High Court means either a District Registry (attached to a county court) or the Royal Courts of Justice in London). There are restrictions on claims which may be issued in the High Court (see 'Value' overleaf).

Use whichever of the following is appropriate:

'In the ....County Court'
(inserting the name of the court)

or

'In the High Court of Justice........................Division'
(inserting eg. 'Queen's Bench' or 'Chancery' as appropriate)
'............................District Registry'
(inserting the name of the District Registry)

or

'In the High Court of Justice........................Division,
(inserting eg. 'Queen's Bench' or 'Chancery' as appropriate)
Royal Courts of Justice'

Claimant and defendant details

As the person issuing the claim, you are called the 'claimant'; the person you are suing is called the 'defendant'. Claimants who are under 18 years old (unless otherwise permitted by the court) and patients within the meaning of the Mental Health Act 1983, must have a litigation friend to issue and conduct court proceedings on their behalf. Court staff will tell you more about what you need to do if this applies to you.

You must provide the following information about yourself and the defendant according to the capacity in which you are suing and in which the defendant is being sued. When suing or being sued as:-

an individual:

All known forenames and surname, whether Mr, Mrs, Miss, Ms or Other (e.g. Dr) and residential address (**including** postcode and telephone number) in England and Wales. Where the defendant is a proprietor of a business, a partner in a firm or an individual sued in the name of a club or other unincorporated association, the address for service should be the usual or last known place of residence **or** principal place of business of the company, firm or club or other unincorporated association.

Where the individual is:

under 18 write '(a child by Mr Joe Bloggs his litigation friend)' after the name. If the child is conducting proceedings on their own behalf write '(a child)' after the child's name.

a patient within the meaning of the Mental Health Act 1983 write '(by Mr Joe Bloggs his litigation friend)' after the patient's name.

trading under another name

you must add the words 'trading as' and the trading name e.g. 'Mr John Smith trading as Smith's Groceries'.

suing or being sued in a representative capacity

you must say what that capacity is e.g. 'Mr Joe Bloggs as the representative of Mrs Sharon Bloggs (deceased)'.

suing or being sued in the name of a club or other unincorporated association

add the words 'suing/sued on behalf of' followed by the name of the club or other unincorporated association.

a firm

enter the name of the firm followed by the words 'a firm' e.g. 'Bandbox - a firm' and an address for service which is either a partner's residential address or the principal or last known place of business.

a corporation (other than a company)

enter the full name of the corporation and the address which is either its principal office **or** any other place where the corporation carries on activities and which has a real connection with the claim.

a company registered in England and Wales

enter the name of the company and an address which is either the company's registered office **or** any place of business that has a real, or the most, connection with the claim e.g. the shop where the goods were bought.

an overseas company (defined by s744 of the Companies Act 1985)

enter the name of the company and either the address registered under s691 of the Act **or** the address of the place of business having a real, or the most, connection with the claim.

N1A - w3 Notes for claimant (4.99)

DEBT RECOVERY

Brief details of claim

Note: The facts and full details about your claim and whether or not you are claiming interest, should be set out in the 'particulars of claim' (see note under 'Particulars of Claim').

You must set out under **this** heading:

* a concise statement of the nature of your claim
* the remedy you are seeking e.g. payment of money; an order for return of goods or their value; an order to prevent a person doing an act; damages for personal injuries.

Value

If you are claiming a **fixed amount of money** (a 'specified amount') write the amount in the box at the bottom right-hand corner of the claim form against 'amount claimed'.

If you are not claiming a fixed amount of money (an 'unspecified amount') under 'Value' write "I expect to recover" followed by whichever of the following applies to your claim:

* "not more than £5,000 **or**
* "more than £5,000 but not more than £15,000" **or**
* "more than £15,000"

If you are **not able** to put a value on your claim, write "I cannot say how much I expect to recover".

Personal injuries

If your claim is for 'not more than £5,000' and includes a claim for personal injuries, you must also write "My claim includes a claim for personal injuries and the amount I expect to recover as damages for pain, suffering and loss of amenity is" followed by either:

* "not more than £1,000" **or**
* "more than £1,000"

Housing disrepair

If your claim is for 'not more than £5,000' and includes a claim for housing disrepair relating to residential premises, you must also write "My claim includes a claim against my landlord for housing disrepair relating to residential premises. The cost of the repairs or other work is estimated to be" followed by either:

* "not more than £1,000" **or**
* "more than £1,000"

If within this claim, you are making a claim for other damages, you must also write:

"I expect to recover as damages" followed by either:

* "not more than £1,000" **or**
* "more than £1,000"

Issuing in the High Court

You may only issue in the High Court if one of the following statements applies to your claim:-

"By law, my claim must be issued in the High Court. The Act which provides this is ....(specify Act)"

or

"I expect to recover more than £15,000"

or

"My claim includes a claim for personal injuries and the value of the claim is £50,000 or more"

or

"My claim needs to be in a specialist High Court list, namely.................................(state which list)".

If one of the statements does apply and you wish to, or must by law, issue your claim in the High Court, write the words "I wish my claim to issue in the High Court because" followed by the relevant statement e.g. "I wish my claim to issue in the High Court because my claim includes a claim for personal injuries and the value of my claim is £50,000 or more."

Defendant's name and address

Enter in this box the full names and address of the defendant receiving the claim form (ie. one claim form for each defendant). If the defendant is to be served outside England and Wales, you may need to obtain the court's permission.

Particulars of claim

You may include your particulars of claim on the claim form in the space provided or in a separate document which you should head 'Particulars of Claim'. It should include the names of the parties, the court, the claim number and your address for service and also contain a statement of truth. You should keep a copy for yourself, provide one for the court and one for each defendant. Separate particulars of claim can either be served

* with the claim form **or**
* within 14 days after the date on which the claim form was served.

If your particulars of claim are served separately from the claim form, they must be served with the forms on which the defendant may reply to your claim.

Your particulars of claim must include

* a concise statement of the facts on which you rely
* a statement (if applicable) to the effect that you are seeking aggravated damages or exemplary damages
* details of any interest which you are claiming
* any other matters required for your type of claim as set out in the relevant practice direction

Address for documents

Insert in this box the address at which you wish to receive documents and/or payments, if different from the address you have already given under the heading 'Claimant'. The address must be in England or Wales. If you are willing to accept service by DX, fax or e-mail, add details.

Statement of truth

This must be signed by you, by your solicitor or your litigation friend, as appropriate.

Where the claimant is a registered company or a corporation the claim must be signed by either the director, treasurer, secretary, chief executive, manager or other officer of the company or (in the case of a corporation) the mayor, chairman, president or town clerk.

Statement of Means

You can ask the debtor to complete this form voluntarily at any stage, or you can use the form as the basis of questions if you get an **order to obtain information**.

The law on data protection restricts the use that can be made of information of the kind you are seeking here. In particular, data must be 'adequate, relevant and not excessive to the purpose for which it is obtained'. We have worded the note at the top of the form on the basis that you will use the information solely in connection with the recovery of money owed to you. If this is not the case, you should contact the Data Protection Registrar (details in 'Useful contacts').

Statement of Means

We will use any information you supply to us on this form exclusively in connection with the recovery of money which you owe us, and will otherwise treat it as confidential.

1   PERSONAL DETAILS

Debtor's name ....

Address ....

Telephone .... (day) .... (evening)

Age ....

Status: married/cohabiting/single/other (please specify) ....

Number of children .... Ages of children ....

Other dependants ....

2   EMPLOYMENT STATUS

2.1   Employed

Employer's name ....

Employer's address ....

Job title ....

Annual wage or salary ....

2.2   Self-employed

Name of business ....

Business address ....

Nature of business ....

Annual earnings ....

2.3   Unemployed

Nature of last job ....

Length of time out of work ....

2.4   Pension

Name of pension provider(s) ....

Annual amount of pension(s) ....

2.5   Other ....

3   ASSETS

3.1   Home

Do you own your own home? Yes/No
If yes:

>   Are you the sole owner? or co-owner? ....

>   Value of home ....

Amount of mortgage ....

Name of mortgage lender ....

3.2 Vehicles

Do you own a car or other motor vehicles? Yes/No

If yes, please complete the following details for each vehicle you own:

Make ....

Registration no. ....

Is vehicle on finance? Yes/No

If yes, please give details in section 4, below.

3.3 Bank details

Do you have a bank account? Yes/No

If yes, please complete the following details for each account:

	1	2
Bank name	....	....
Bank address	....	....
Account name	....	....
Account number	....	....
Balance	....	....

3.4 Savings and investments

Do you have any savings or investments? Yes/No

If yes, please provide details including value ....

....

3.5 Property

Do you own property other than your home? Yes/No

If yes, please provide the following details for each property:

	1	2
Are you the sole owner or co-owner?	....	....
Value of home	....	....
Amount of mortgage (if any)	....	....
Name of mortgage lender	....	....

3.6 Pensions

Do you or your employer pay into a pension scheme? Yes/No

If yes, please give details ....

Do you receive income from a pension which you have not declared at 2.4? If so, please give details here ....

....

3.7 Other assets
Please provide details of any other assets you own, e.g. boats, jewellery, works of art etc. ....

....

3.8 Money owed to you
Does anybody owe you money? Yes/No
If yes, please give details of the debtor(s) and amount(s)

	1	2	3
Debtor			
Amount			

4 LIABILITIES

Please give details of money you owe, for example:

4.1 Credit card debts

	1	2	3
Name and address of lender			
Amount owed			
Monthly instalment			

4.2 Hire purchase
(please complete for each hire purchase arrangement you have)

	1	2	3
Name and address of lender			
Amount owed			
Monthly instalment			

4.3 Finance on vehicles
(please complete for each vehicle subject to finance)

	1	2	3
Name and address of lender			
Amount owed			
Monthly instalment			

4.4 Catalogue debts
(please complete for each debt)

	1	2	3
Lender			
Amount owed			
Weekly/monthly instalment			

4.5   County court judgments
(please complete for each judgment)

	1	2	3
Creditor			
Amount owed			
Monthly instalment			

4.6   Bank loans
(but excluding any mortgage previously mentioned)
(please complete for each loan)

	1	2	3
Lender			
Amount owed			
Monthly instalment			

4.7   Any other debts
(please complete for each debt)

	1	2	3
Lender			
Amount owed			
Weekly/monthly instalment			

5   MONTHLY INCOME AND EXPENDITURE

A   Income

Wages or salary after tax and NI	£ .... per week/month
Pension	£ .... per week/month
Other income	£ .... per week/month
Partner's net wages or salary	£ .... per week/month
Child benefit	£ .... per week/month
State income (please specify)	£ .... per week/month
Maintenance	£ .... per week/month

Other (please specify)

....	£ .... per week/month
....	£ .... per week/month
....	£ .... per week/month

B   Expenditure

Mortgage or rent	£ .... per week/month
Gas/electricity	£ .... per week/month
Telephone	£ .... per week/month
Insurances (please specify)	£ .... per week/month
Pension contributions	£ .... per week/month

Travel (public transport)	£ .... per week/month
Car expenses	£ .... per week/month
Food	£ .... per week/month
Council tax	£ .... per week/month
Water rates	£ .... per week/month
Other (please specify)	£ .... per week/month
....	£ .... per week/month
....	£ .... per week/month
Total expenditure	£ .... per week/month

C   Other payments

Add up any weekly/monthly instalments from
section 4 and enter the total here)   £ .... per week/month

Disposable income

Income (A)	£_____per week/month
less	
Expenditure (B+C)	£_____per week/month
Balance	£_____per week/month

I confirm this as an accurate record of my/our financial affairs
at *(date)*.

Signed ....

Creditor's Bankruptcy Petition (form 6.7)

Form 6.7 is the Bankruptcy Petition to use where the debtor has failed to comply with a statutory demand for a debt payable immediately. This is by far the most common situation, but there are other situations and other forms to cover them. Look on the Insolvency Service website and take professional advice if you think this applies to you.

Nowhere, either on the Insolvency Service website or elsewhere on the web, have we found an idiot's guide to completing form 6.7. The marginal notes on the form are mostly straightforward, but we have added a few notes here which you may find helpful.

Rule 6.6

Form 6.7

Creditor's Bankruptcy Petition on Failure to Comply with a Statutory Demand for a Liquidated Sum Payable Immediately (Title)

(a) insert full names(s) and address(es) of petitioner(s)

I/We (a)_____

(b) insert full name, place of residence and occupation (if any) of debtor

petition the court that a bankruptcy order may be made against (b)_____

(c) insert in full any other name(s) by which the debtor is or has been known

[also known as (c)_____]

(d) insert trading name (adding "with another or others", if this is so), business address and nature of business

[and carrying on business as (d)_____]

(e) insert any other address or addresses at which the debtor has resided at or after the time the petition debt was incurred

[and lately residing at (e)_____]

(f) Give the same details as specified in note (d) above for any other businesses which have been carried on at or after the time the petition debt was incurred

[and lately carrying on business as (f)_____]

and say as follows:-

(a) You are the *petitioner*. Put your name and address here.

(b) Here you write the name and home address and occupation of the debtor.

(c) Here you add any other names by which the debtor is known (for example, Rosy Border is also known as Rosemary Rabson and Rosemary Border Rabson).

(d) You would only add this if the debtor was in business.

(e) and (f) Only fill in 'and lately residing at/lately carrying on business as' if the debtor has recently changed address or occupation.

(g) Delete as applicable

1. (g) [The debtor's centre of main interests has been][The debtor has had an establishment] at _____

OR

The debtor carries on business as an insurance undertaking; a credit institution; an investment undertaking providing services involving the holding of funds or securities for third parties; or a collective investment undertaking as referred to in Article 1.2 of the EC Regulation

OR

The debtor's centre of main interests is not within a Member State

---

Clause 1

The first part is for business debtors. The answer could well be the same as for (d). Delete anything that does not apply.

(h) Or as the case may be following the terms of Rule 6.9

2. The debtor has for the greater part of six months immediately preceding the presentation of this petition (g) [resided at] [carried on business at]

....

within the district of this court (h)

Under the EC Regulation:
(i) The centre of main interests should correspond to the place where the debtor conducts the administration of his interests on a regular basis.
(ii) Establishment is defined as "any place of operations where the debtor caries out a non-transitory economic activity with human means and goods".

Clause 2

Here you say where the debtor has lived (or carried on business) for the last six months. This is to make sure that the debtor comes within the jurisdiction of the court to which you are applying.

3. The debtor is justly and truly indebted to me [us] in the aggregate sum of

£(j)..............

4. The above-mentioned debt is for a liquidated sum payable immediately and the debtor appears to be unable to pay it

5. On (k)_____ a statutory demand was served upon the debtor by

(l)_____
in respect of the above-mentioned debt. To the best of my knowledge and belief the demand has neither been complied with nor set aside in accordance with the Rules and no application to set it aside is outstanding

(m)

Clause 3

Here you say what the debt is for.

Clause 4

This says the money is payable now and the debtor seems unable to pay.

Clause 5

Here you say when you issued the statutory demand. You must say how the statutory demand was served (for example, by personal service) and when it was served – before or after 1700 on Monday to Friday, or any time on Saturday or Sunday.

Ignore note (m) unless for some reason you are petitioning for bankruptcy before the three-week period from service of the statutory demand has elapsed.

6. I/We do not, nor does any person on my/our behalf, hold any security on the debtor's estate, or any part thereof, for the payment of the above-mentioned sum

OR

I/We hold security for the payment of (g) [part of] the above-mentioned sum. I/We will give up such security for the benefit of all the creditors in the event of a bankruptcy order being made.

OR

I/We hold security for the payment of part of the above-mentioned sum and I/we estimate the value of such security to be £   . This petition is not made in respect of the secured part of my/our debt.

Clause 6

Here you say whether or not you hold any security: normally you won't.

Endorsement

The court will fill in the hearing details: leave blank.

You are a litigant in person, so you can delete the solicitor's details.

Note: the following certificate must be added at the bottom of the form

'I/we certify that on (date) I/we attended the (name) County Court and was/were informed by an officer of the court that no money had been paid into court in the action or matter (name) v (name) claim no (fill in if you have one) pursuant to the Statutory Demand'.

Winding-up petition

Creditors' winding-up petitions where the creditor is not represented by a solicitor are uncommon, but the form is available online at www.insolvency.gov.uk.

Too much is at stake to risk getting your paperwork wrong. Get it checked by a court official, who will know how their own district judge likes things presented.

Note that the information required about debtor companies (company number, date of incorporation, registered office, etc) is freely available over the telephone from Companies House (see 'Useful contacts').

The Endorsement is left blank for the court to set the hearing date.

Form 4.2

Rule 4.7

Winding-Up Petition

Form 4.2

(Title)   **(Registered No.   )**

(a) Insert title of court

To (a)

(b) Insert full name(s) and address(es) of petitioner(s)

The petition of (b)

(c) Insert full name and registered no. of company subject to petition

1. (c)

(hereinafter called "the company") was incorporated on

(d) Insert date of incorporation

(d)

under the Companies Act 19

(e) Insert address of registered office

2. The registered office of the company is at (e)

(f) Insert amount of nominal capital and how it is divided

3. The nominal capital of the company is (f) £
divided into   shares of £   each. The amount of the capital paid up or credited as paid up is (g) £

(g) Insert amount of capital paid up or credited as paid up

4. The principal objects for which the company was established are as follows:

and other objects stated in the memorandum of association of the company

(h) Set out the grounds on which a winding-up order is sought

5. (h)

(j) Delete as applicable

6. The company (j) is/is not an insurance undertaking; a credit institution; an investment undertaking providing services involving the holding of funds or securities for third parties; or a collective investment undertaking as referred to in Article 1.2 of the EC Regulation.

(k) Insert name of person swearing affidavit

7. For the reasons stated in the affidavit of (k)   filed in support here of it is considered that the EC Regulation on insolvency proceedings (j) will/will not apply (j) and that these proceedings will be (l)_____ proceedings as defined in Article 3 of the EC Regulation

(l) Insert whether main, secondary or territorial proceedings

8. In the circumstances it is just and equitable that the company should be wound up
The petitioner(s) therefore pray(s) as follows:-

(1) that (c)

may be wound up by the court under the provisions of the Insolvency Act 1986
or
(2) that such other order may be made as the court thinks fit

Note: It is intended to serve this petition on (m) [the company] [and]

Endorsement

This petition having been presented to the court

on _____ will be heard at (n) [Royal Courts of Justice, Strand, London, WC2A 2LL] [(n) _____ County Court
_____]

[(o) _____ District Registry
_____]

on:

Date_____

Time _____hours
(or as soon thereafter as the petition can be heard)

The solicitor to the petitioner is:-

Name_____

Address_____

_____

Telephone no_____

Reference_____

(j) [Whose London Agents are:-

Name_____

Address_____

_____

Telephone no. _____

Reference_____

Official forms

The forms mentioned in this book come from three sources: the Court Service, the Land Registry and the Insolvency Service. We have included copies of the main ones here, to give you an idea of how they look. Additionally we provide worked examples of the most important ones.

Court Service forms are available from any court or from the Court Service website. You are free to download as many copies of the forms as you wish.

Land Registry – we mention SIM, OC1, AN1, UN1, RX1 and K1. These forms are available from the Land Registry or online from their website (see 'Useful contacts').

Insolvency Service forms are available from local Citizens Advice Bureaux (CABs) and online from the Insolvency Service website.

Here is a list of forms:

Court Service forms

Fee remission

EX 160

Claim

N1	Claim Form
N1A	Notes for Claimant on Completing a Claim Form
N1C	Notes for Defendant on Replying to the Claim Form
N215	Certificate of Service (*if you serve the Claim Form yourself*)
N9	Response Pack for Defendant (Acknowledgment of Service)

N9A   Admission (specified amount)

N9B   Defence and Counterclaim

N150   Allocation Questionnaire *(to enable the court to decide which track the case should go on)*

N20   Witness Summons

N244   Application Notice *(used if applying for **summary judgment**)*

*Note that you apply for a **default judgment** using the bottom half of the Notice of Issue (Specified Amount) and Request for Judgment which the court sends you; it is not online.*

Enforcement: order to obtain information

N316   Application for Order that Debtor Attend Court for Questioning

N316A Application for Order that Officer of Debtor Company Attend Court for Questioning

EX140 Record of Examination (individual)

EX141 Record of Examination (officer of company or corporation)

Enforcement: Warrant of Execution

N323   Request for Warrant of Execution

N445   Request for Reissue of Warrant

Enforcement: Attachment of Earnings

N337   Request for Attachment of Earnings Order

N336   Request and Result of Search in the Attachment of Earnings

N446   Request for Reissue of Enforcement or Oral Examination (not Warrant) *(used to reinstate an Attachment of Earnings Order)*

Enforcement: Third Party Debt Order

N349   Application for Third Party Debt Order

Enforcement: Charging Order

N379   Application for Charging Order on Land or Property

N380   Application for Charging Order on Securities

N86   Interim Charging Order

N244   Application Notice *(used for applying for a Charging Order when there is more than one owner of the property or securities)*

Insolvency Service forms

Bankruptcy

6.1   Statutory Demand *(no judgment debt)*

6.2   Statutory Demand *(where there is already a judgment debt)*

6.11   Affidavit of Personal Service of Statutory Demand

6.7   Creditor's Bankruptcy Petition

6.13   Affidavit of Truth of Statements in Bankruptcy Petition

6.17   Affidavit of Personal Service of Bankruptcy Petition

Liquidation

4.1   Statutory Demand

4.2   Winding-up Petition

4.3   Affidavit Verifying Winding-up Petition

4.4   Affidavit of Service of Winding-up Petition at Registered Office

4.5   Affidavit of Service of Winding-up Petition Other than at Registered Office or on an Overseas Company

4.6   Advertisement of Winding-up Petition

4.7   Certificate that Relevant Rules have been Complied With

Useful contacts

Department for Constitutional Affairs (previously Lord Chancellor's Department)

Civil Procedure Rules – the paper version is expensive, but you can access the CPR online.

Website: www.dca.gov.uk/civil/procrules_fin/

Money Claim Online

Customer Help Desk: 0845 601 5935

Website: www.courtservice.gov.uk/mcol

Court Service

The Court Service is an executive agency of the Department of Constitutional Affairs, which provides administrative support to the High Court and county courts.

The Court Service
Southside
105 Victoria Street
London SW1E 6QT

Tel: 020 7210 2266

Website: www.courtservice.gov.uk

Your local court, and probably your Citizens Advice Bureau (CAB) too, will have copies of all the forms and leaflets you need. Court staff are ace form-fillers and it is worth getting someone there to check your paperwork before you file it.

The Court Service website (see above) has all the forms and guidance leaflets online, together with details of courts: addresses, telephone numbers – some even offer a virtual tour of their premises.

We have mentioned a few Court Service leaflets in this book. A complete list is available online. Here are the ones relevant to debt recovery.

EX50   *County Court Fees* (fees change and you should always check before taking proceedings)

EX160A *Court Fees – Do You Have To Pay Them?*

EX301   *Making A Claim? Some Questions To Ask Yourself*

EX2   *How To Start A Claim*

EX304   *No Reply To My Claim Form – What Should I Do?*

EX306   *The Defendant Disputes All Or Part Of My Claim*

EX307   *The Small Claims Track*

EX309   *The Defendant Admits My Claim – I Claimed A Fixed Amount Of Money*

EX321   *I Have A Judgment But The Defendant Hasn't Paid – What Do I Do?*

EX322   *How Do I Ask For A Warrant Of Execution?*

EX323   *How Do I Ask For An Attachment Of Earnings Order?*

EX324   *Orders To Obtain Information – How Do I Apply For An Order?*

EX325   *Third Party Debt Orders And Charging Orders – How Do I Apply For An Order?*

EX341   *I Have Been Asked To Be A Witness – What Do I Do?*

EX342   *Some Things You Should Know About Coming To A Court Hearing*

EX345   *About Bailiffs And Sheriffs' Officers*

EX350   *A Guide To Debt Recovery Through The County Courts For Small Businesses*

Other leaflets

Late Payment Legislation and Interest Calculator (to calculate interest on debts). Available online at www.payontime.co.uk

HM Land Registry

(for charging orders and possibly general sleuthing)

HM Land Registry
32 Lincoln's Inns Fields
London WC2A 3PH

Tel: 0207 917 8888
Land Registry Act Helpline: 0870 90 88 061
Website: www.landreg.gov.uk

Bankruptcy and liquidation

Insolvency Service

Dealing With Debt – How To Make Someone Bankrupt
Available from any Official Receiver's office or online
from:

www.insolvency.gov.uk/information/guidanceleaflets/
debt/makesomeone.htm

*Dealing With Debt – How To Wind Up A Company That
Owes You Money*
Available from any Official Receiver's office or online
from:

www.insolvency.gov.uk/information/guidanceleaflets/
debt/companyowesmoney.htm

There are many other goodies on the Insolvency Service
website: www.insolvency.gov.uk

Individual Insolvency Register

The Individual Insolvency Register keeps details of
bankruptcy and **individual voluntary arrangements**.
You can:
o   go in person to any Official Receiver's office (listed
     in your local telephone directory), fill in a form and
     receive a print-out of the information

○ write to

The Insolvency Service
5th Floor
West Wing
45–46 Stephenson Street
Birmingham B24 UP

You can download a copy of the search form from www.insolvency.gov.uk/pdfs/insolvencyregister.pdf

The **Insolvency Service Disqualified Directors Hotline** was set up 'to catch defiant directors and undischarged bankrupts who blatantly disregard disqualification orders made against them'. It is open 24 hours a day and will tell you free of charge whether someone is on their list of people who are disqualified from acting as company directors.

Tel: 0845 601 3546

Website: www.insolvency.gov.uk/ourservices/hotline/disquali.htm

Insolvency Service Helpline (general)

Tel: 0207 637 1110

They can tell you whether a company has gone into **compulsory liquidation** or is subject to liquidation proceedings, or has entered into a **company voluntary arrangement** (CVA). There is no charge.

There is also a central enquiry line which provides initial information on insolvency legislation and procedures, including details of the work of the Official Receiver.

Tel: 0207 291 6895

Companies House: the Central Index (of company winding-up petitions)

To check to see if someone else has already filed a winding-up petition, search the Central Index which is maintained by Companies House.

Companies House has seven offices in England, Wales and Scotland. Its headquarters are in Cardiff.

Companies House
Crown Way
Cardiff CF14 3UZ

General enquiries: 0870 333 3636

Companies House also maintains a register of disqualified directors. Ring the general enquiries number above and give them the person's surname and initial; they can usually check over the telephone. This is a free service.

They will also provide full details (addresses, occupations, dates of appointment, etc) of *existing company directors* for £4 per company if you want the results posted, or £5 if you want them faxed. Alternatively, you can access information on their website: www.companieshouse gov.uk

The Disqualified Directors Hotline (see above) is another way of checking on disqualified directors.

Insolvency in London

Bankruptcy Court
Royal Courts of Justice
Thomas More Building
The Strand
London WC2A 2LL

Tel: 020 7947 6294

The Companies Court *(for liquidations)*
Room TM 209
Royal Courts of Justice
Thomas More Building
The Strand
London WC2A 2LL

Tel: 020 7947 6294

London Gazette

To advertise your winding-up petition:

London Gazette
PO Box 7293
London SE1 5ZH

Tel: 020 7394 4580
Website: www.gazettes-online.co.uk

You can advertise online or over the telephone on 0207 873 8308 (direct line to their Advertising Manager) using your credit card.

The cost of a single insertion is £36.80 (inclusive of VAT) – cheques are payable to *London Gazette*. Give at least two days' notice of the date you wish the advertisement to appear.

General

Yellow Pages/Talking Pages

Most people are only issued with Yellow Pages for their own area. Call Talking Pages on 0800 600 900 for a free nationwide trawl.

Data Protection Registrar

Wycliffe House
Water Lane
Wilmslow
Cheshire SK9 5AF

Information line: 01625 545745
Notification line: 01625545740
Switchboard: 01625 545700
Fax: 01625 524510

Email : data@dataprotection.gov.uk
Website: www dataprotection.gov.uk

Register of County Court Judgments

This is maintained by
Registry Trust Limited
173/175 Cleveland Street
London W1P 5PE

Tel: 020 7380 0133

For £4.50 a name (make out the cheque to Registry Trust Limited) you can get a print-out of any judgments against that name. You can also download an application form from their website at www.registry-trust.org.uk, complete the form on screen, print and mail.

Index

Notes

Notes

Notes

Notes

DEBT RECOVERY